Walking in the Light

Walking in the Light

A Spiritual Guide to the Universe

and our Place within it

Carol Maxine Statham

In the interest of privacy, names may have been changed or excluded.

Disclaimer notice

Please note the information contained within this book is for educational and entertainment purposes only. No warranties of any kind are expressed or implied. Readers acknowledge that the author is not engaging in the rendering of legal, financial, medical, or professional advice. Please consult a licensed professional before attempting any techniques outlined in this book. By reading this book the reader agrees that under no circumstances is the author responsible for any losses, direct or

ISBN 978-1-3999-1940-1

Dedication

For My Family

With Love.

Acknowledgements

This book would not have taken place if not for the invaluable input, support and encouragement from my Spirit Squad, my editor, and my darling husband all of whom I shall be eternally grateful.

Edited by Dr Nicholas John Bennett: MBBChir, PhD.

Table of Contents

Introduction.

The early years.

I am a Spiritual medium/healer and professional astrologer. In all these disciplines, I work in the service of Spirit. But it has not been an easy journey. I was the eldest of three, born on 5th November in 1948 known as Guy Fawkes Day or bonfire night in Great Britain- a happy child full of exuberance and mischief as befitting a firework display! As a young man, my dad had been in the Royal Air Force, and later trained as a draughtsman in civvy life. He was a kind, gentle man who loved his family dearly. Mum was the opposite, she could whiplash you verbally, and if that did not work, she would lash out physically. In today's world she would be labelled an abuser, but when I was a child society just seem to accept things like that. I also think dad probably mitigated her behaviour. He would never speak ill of anyone thus he could never see the great harm his wife was doing to her children, and the family unit. It might be assumed, therefore, that my early life was fractured, but this was not so. Apart from having a close relationship with my dad, I was also close to my grandparents, both paternal and maternal, and there were cousins that I saw on regular occasions ensuring a sense of close-knit family. But my other saving grace, beginning at the age of three, is that I have always been acutely aware of "another world". A world made known to me through mental visitations, and words conveyed to me not heard by the physical ear.

Initiation into this "other world" began on the day I had been cycling on my little tricycle and decided for some irrational reason to stick my fingers up inside the hollow handlebars! Brought out the house by my screams, my visiting maternal grandfather scooped me up, bike and all and rushed me back into the house to plonk me on the wooden draining board of the Belfast sink. With my mother and grandmother hovering in the background, my screams persisted as he attempted to loosen my fingers with warm soapy water. Then suddenly, this other lady appeared as if from nowhere! Although I did not know her, her appearance did not frighten me, but instead induced a sense of calm.

I heard her say to me, "There, there, don't wriggle so. Soon your fingers will be free again, and you can ask your grandad for an ice lolly!" Then she was gone as soon as she came, and my fingers were free.

I looked across to my mum and asked for an ice lolly, at which she rhetorically asked, "Where are we going to get an ice lolly from?" but just as grandad was putting me back down on the floor, the chiming of an ice cream van could be heard in our street.

"This lass is psychic," said Grandad, "we had better watch her!"

What made this event remarkable, as far as my family were concerned, is that it is doubtful I could have known what an ice lolly was, I had never had one before! And although we lived on the Dorset coast at the time, ice cream vans were not very common, at least not on our street. And so, my relationship with my lady friend had begun. She was a constant companion, popping up in my mind's eye throughout my early life, tutoring me with life lessons that could not be found in a conventional classroom. She was my saviour, my helpmate, my consoling companion following another beating or hard slap across the face with the words, "you little bitch" from my mother.

Seven years following my initiation of the Spiritual realm I was to discover who she was. On the day of my paternal grandfather's funeral, I had gone into my grandparent's bedroom, a room that was normally out of bounds! I was close to my grandfather, very close, and wanted to be close again. The last time I had seen this room, my grandfather had been laying in his bed dying of lung cancer. As my eyes scanned the room, they rested on a photo in a silver frame. It was a photo of a young woman dressed in what looked like a nurse's uniform. I had not recalled ever seeing it before. As I stood looking down at it, my grandmother suddenly walked in the room.

Before she could tell me off for being there, I quickly asked, "who is this lady"?

Taking the silver frame from my hand, my grandmother was to tell me she was my grandfather's mother, my great grandmother, Mary Anne Cheek. As a young woman, my lady friend had been a nurse and professional midwife which would explain her caring, but practical personality. The exhilaration that hit my solar plexus that day has been with me ever since. The recognition not only of another world, but the recognition that somehow, I could acknowledge it, and it acknowledged me. My lady friend was to stay with me for many years, appearing when I needed help, or at my mother's home confinement when my little brother was born, which I had the good fortune to witness. At 12 years old, a maternal bond surged through my body that day as my little brother lay cradled in my arms, just a few minutes old. It was a bond that was to be deep and lasting, right up to the present day. In later years too, my lady friend appeared at the birth of my son Daniel. Soon over the years, as I started growing up, my paternal grandfather from the "other side" would join her in my tutoring from the Spiritual World.

Growing up.

My parents were restless people, constantly moving to a new house, either within the confines of the West Country of England or emigrating to Australia and back again. The constant disruption to my formal education meant it was basic, which was not helped by my parent's lack of interest, particularly my mother, in the educational welfare of their children. But my saving grace was my creative eye. I had always been good at art, crafts and writing. When I left school at 15, armed only with an art portfolio, my dad talked me into applying for a three-year apprenticeship at the aircraft and defence factory where he was employed. I had never heard of a Technical Tracer before, but it was to be a successful career, one that spanned over 22 years. In the early days, it gave me the financial independence I so desperately sought as my mother's attacks on me became more severe, leaving me no choice but to leave home at the age of 18. Over the years I led a rather conventional life, fitting into a routine of work, rest, and play. There were marriages, divorce and tears, and house moves around Great Britain. But my greatest joy came with the birth of my 3 beautiful children. These years also brought a different attitude towards the Spiritual realm. I had become sucked into a secular material world which led me to question my Spiritual experiences. Was I mad? Did I really have a wicked imagination as my mother claimed? Were my experiences pure fantasy and fabrication? And so, I became complacent, even playing Devil's advocate with the Spiritual forces. I remember on one occasion following a warning from the Spiritual realm, saying out loud, "Oh for goodness' sake leave me alone. I just want to live my life." Consequently, although full of joy on the one hand, these years were full of heartache, challenges, and painful lessons. Now I know it is okay to question our Spiritual experiences, because that is how we grow Spiritually.

The middle years.

My conventional world came tumbling in on me in 1992, when several life changing events impacted my life, including a car crash which produced a near-death experience, juxtaposing quite separately (or so I thought) the passing of my darling brother. I had taken my children to the local swimming baths and was driving back home after the event. Approaching a familiar tight corner in the narrow Somerset country lane, I had slowed right down, preparing myself for the bend before me. Just at that point, I was engulfed in this enormous tunnel of White Light, pure and dazzling, and I seemed unable to stop myself being sucked into it. Then I saw my brother descending before me.

I remember calling out to him, "Please do not go, wait for me."

Then I heard a voice, a voice without form which was firm and gentle telling me, "I had to go back," and that "it was not my time." The next thing I recall is the noise of an engine, and the smell of oil - paraphernalia of a crashed car and a child whimpering. My mind had blanked, and I had driven through a solid stone wall into the garden of a man, who five minutes earlier had been cutting his lawn. The Angels were in the area that day, protecting everyone involved. My children only suffered seatbelt burns, and my injuries were minor compared to what might have happened, enabling me to leave hospital after a week.

I had only been home for a few days when I received a house call from two police officers. Believing it was about my road accident, what they told me shook me to the core. My darling brother had been found dead in his flat. He had started drinking at the age of 15, discovering alcohol helped him cope with a debilitating stutter, only to pass away 16 years later with cirrhosis of the liver. It was believed his body had been there for at least a week making it possible he died on the day of my road accident. For many years I had "seen" his physical death approaching, believing that if I warned him, I could stop it happening. Only in later years, did my husband tell me, that if I could "see" it happening, then perhaps I could not stop it. I have never felt such pain, before or since. It felt as if my heart had been ripped out, and yet I had been told by the Tunnel of Light to go on living.

From that day till now, my Spiritual experiences became more pronounced and meaningful, not so much as a Spiritual Awakening, but more of a Spiritual Reawakening. These events were to open the door even wider to another dimension, a dimension that I had tried to ignore, leaving me floundering between two worlds. Now I knew I could no longer ignore the Spiritual realm, my brother "on the other side" was to see to that!

The Irish years.

Following instruction by my Spirit guides, my husband and I moved to Ireland in the summer of 1998. Now an Irish citizen living in county Clare, I have taken a different path. Encouraged by my husband, Dermot, I have gained a BA honour in the Humanities from the Open University, and studied the theory and practices of reflexology, aromatherapy, mediumship, Spiritual healing, and of course astrologer. These are subjects' science cannot explain, but those of us that avail of them know they work. Rejuvenated and empowered with my newfound information, learning of universal laws, for the first time in my life, it became clear who I was and who I did not want to be. All of this was clarified by my father's sister, who divulged to me that two great aunts had been Spiritual mediums, a gift she said, I had inherited. At the age of 52, this was the first time I had ever heard this information. And so, over the last 21 years I have learnt that there are greater forces at work that have nothing to do with the material world. It is a Life Force, a Super Consciousness which is Supernatural, that weaves itself through all life forms, including Homo sapiens. Mankind is but one species of a Super Nature that is governed and regulated by cosmic law and order that, for the time being, conventional science cannot explain.

For many years I have worked keeping a low profile as an independent practitioner. These were learning years for me, as

I developed my skills and craft, until in 2015 I was informed by my Spirit guides I must write a book. They wanted me to reach greater numbers of people. They gave me the title of each chapter, then told me to go away and research. Researching these topics made me realise that I am not alone in my experiences, there are many others like me, both historically and in the present day, including academics and scientists. And so, in its original form, the book had 26 chapters, making it far too large and complicated for any publisher to be interested in! And here I am grateful to my eldest son Nicholas, who was at a point undergoing his own midlife crisis, offered to edit my book into the polished version we have today. As a child we used to call him "the Prof" because of his leanings to scientific research and understanding. But like his mum, he was also sensitive to the undercurrents of "another world." Having studied medicine at Cambridge, he became Associate Professor of Paediatrics and a Medical Director of infectious diseases. For a moment in time, life was successful and rewarding, both in the material sense, and in his career. But the demands he placed on himself, or by which were placed on him by others to reach Ego incentive objectives, were impossible to meet causing him to lose sight of what was important in life. Just when I needed him, he needed me showing the cosmic law of synchronicity! Reading my book reminded him of his Spiritual component and helped him reset his priority list, which is interesting, because that is exactly why my book was written.

With our beautiful planet beset with so many problems created by human action, and now the global COVID-19 pandemic and climate crisis, my Spirit Guides and the Angels inform me it is time for all humanity to reset their priority list. In fact, there are many already doing so as more and more people become involved in climate action, environmentalists, conservationists, oceanography, and animal welfare. There is a heightened Spiritual awareness that humanity cannot go on like this. Globally we see Spirit and the Ego fighting for supremacy, and the outcome will determine the future of the planet and all life thereof.

And so, I have written this book for several reasons. First, I want to show that there are forces at work that have nothing to do with our material world, the political, economic and the financial institutions that fuel everything, and the Ego incentive objectives of human action. I want to show that all life on planet Earth has a Spiritual component and is equal in consideration. And secondly, I want to share my own experiences of the Spiritual realm, and why I am so convinced of an afterlife, and all the valuable lessons that came with that. Your loved ones that have passed over, including your pets are truly never far away. And lastly, I hope by expanding your awareness of this Spiritual component, and the Ego it will encourage more responsibility towards all life on planet Earth, the environment, and the climate. I hope my book will show that our actions really matter. By drawing attention to the Spiritual component, I will show that the solution to our well-being, mentally, emotionally, physically, and spiritually and the well-being of the planet lies within all of us.

A word from the Editor

When I offered to help my mum edit this book, it was at a time when I very clearly needed to listen to my own “Spirit Guides”. This is actually her second book, her first of which I was not involved with. But I felt the pull to help her only at this time – perhaps because I could. After leaving my job as a Physician suffering from the physical and mental effects of extreme burnout, I found myself relaxed and creative, and that I could read and write without distraction.

Looking over her sources and reading some of them myself, I was further inspired to help – the book truly drew me in. I realized that I could refine the text without losing the intention or meaning of her work, and even add a little to it, and so we set about collaborating on an editorial process that has taken the better part of a year. Although we have substantially cut the manuscript down from the original 26 chapters (perhaps the remainder will be another book…?) we feel that we have kept the thread of her explanation of Spirit, and its importance to our Past, Present, and Future selves. There are scattered contributions of my own (in particular the chapters related to Spiritual Healing), but this very much remains her book. Consider my contributions as a whetstone, merely polishing the blacksmith's steel.

I have my own tales of the paranormal and unexplained happenings from the age of 7 years old, and being a firmly logical scientist, researcher, and physician, it has obviously been impossible to reconcile what my eyes and ears (and inner voice) have shown me over the years with the teachings of textbooks and the classroom. I have simply come to accept that certain things are inexplicable, and having witnessed them with my mother, and even now with my son Liam (who, according to at least one medium, has also inherited the Gift from his great-great Aunts) I have found a greater balance and meaning in Life, and a sense of peace about what comes next. As Hamlet says in the play, "There are more things in Heaven and Earth, Horatio, than are dreamt of in your philosophy."

"Walking in the Light" will show you some of those things.
Dr Nicholas John Bennett: MBBChir, PhD. 1st February 2021

Chapter 1

The Voice

I once heard it said that research had shown that over 50% of children in the Irish Republic had claimed they have heard voices inside their head, and that medical evaluation concluded that these children mostly grew out of this period and that those that did not were psychologically disturbed.[1] I found this report horrifying in its implications, since it leaves me to conclude that "this period" bore no substance to reality and was considered a figment of the child's imagination. In contrast, research from Manchester University in the UK concluded that hearing voices is not necessarily a symptom of mental illness. It was found that many people admitted to hearing voices entering their mind that came from outside themselves and have never felt the need to seek advice professionally regarding their mental state. [2]

This Manchester study goes on to inform us that in Holland one in twenty-five people regularly hear voices. For some people, the voice inside their mind created distress. For others, it was a very positive experience. Either way, the voice seemed to carry a very important message to the hearer. The findings of the research found the onset of hearing voices in more than 70% of people was triggered after experiencing a traumatic life event. [2] As a Spiritual Medium, this piece of information made me think. Does experiencing a traumatic event trigger the opening of a door? We very often hear of people surviving a near death situation which provokes a turning point in their life. Others may experience or witness a traumatic event that provokes what they come to understand as "a Spiritual

Awakening". Whatever way the trauma is felt, the experience seems to unlock a spirit portal, a doorway into an ethereal world that had gone undetected beforehand. This begs the question, is the "voice inside our head" a figment of imagination or an independent entity that makes itself known to us and comes to our aid only when it seems appropriate to do so? Sigmund Freud argues the voice is a psychological aid that makes itself known to us when we need help, reassurance, or companionship. In other words, it is an invention of the mind, a safety net that protects us from shock or hurt or loneliness that we may be experiencing.[2]

I have been hearing voices inside my head for as long as I can remember. This was my life's biggest secret. Fear of ridicule or being labelled mentally unstable dictated I did not divulge the information to anyone until after my brother had passed over, and even then, it was only to my third husband. The previous decade or so bore witness to my brother's long struggle with alcohol addiction. It had destroyed him and his life, and in his last two years I had struggled with the psychic knowledge and vision of his youthful physical demise. It was like bearing witness to the slow suicide of someone you dearly love. When I heard his voice, which was separate from my thinking self, informing me he had died, I experienced an excruciating pain in my heart. Forty years of experiencing voices inside my head, combined with Spiritual and psychic visitations gave me the surety that this voice and its message was real. Yet the sister in me did not want to hear or know. My first reaction on hearing my brother's voice was to recoil from the news in a state of profound excruciating emotional pain and denial. Like a wounded animal, I could not bring myself to visit his flat where he lived to check this information out in the days that followed. Instead, the news of his physical demise was brought to me by the police a week later. It was thought he had been dead in his flat for about a week. He was thirty-one years old, and I was forty-three. His passing was indeed a very traumatic event for me, a turning point in my life, the impact of which dictated a completely different Life Path.

The voices which visit external from my thinking are mostly, but not always, accompanied with visitations of family members who have passed over. Their voices from the "other side" are the same as they were when they lived in the profane world, using the same vocabulary and speech style. Other times, the voices come from complete strangers, again accompanied with visitations of what these people look like. Other times, the voice comes from a celestial being, an Angel, sometimes just a bright light, not always visiting me with a visitation of form, but identified by a female or male voice that sounds old English and formal, yet profoundly comforting, compassionate and full of wisdom. The voice of our Guardian Angel will be of the like. The voice of God, according to the Angels is the collective force of goodness and will be in the modern vernacular, deep and gentle, very casual but to the point, like a good male friend. Our Spirit guide will speak to us in the vernacular of their time here on earth but now full of wisdom learnt thereof, both of this world and the "other side". Our Spirit, our higher self sounds like our own voice and is always upbeat and encouraging, always thinking of others in the wider community. Whereas the voice of our Ego, which is our lower self is negative, disparaging, depressive and abusive and always speaks of "I" as opposed to thinking of benefits for the bigger picture. It is egotistical. On all these occasions, the voice is not of my thinking self, it is louder, although softer and more subtle like picking up a message telepathically. Other times it may seem as if the voice is speaking in my left ear although again, I hear it within my head. A psychiatrist may indeed pronounce me needing psychiatric help given my childhood background of a mother, who was at best controlling, critical and spiteful at worse, cruel, and abusive. They may indeed conclude that my experiences of the paranormal and/or the Spiritual Realm are a figment of my imagination to replace the emotional warmth lacking in my childhood or lacking in my relationship with my mother. But this would be far from the truth. Despite my mother's adverse reaction against me, I had a very happy childhood. I never felt devoid of human emotional warmth as my grandparents, aunts and uncles, my darling dad and brother more than made up for the emotional deficiency in my mum. I believe it is far too easy to dismiss things we do not understand in a disparaging fashion, notwithstanding the vagaries of the mind which still evades scientific understanding.

The plain fact is we all, every single one of us, live inside our head. Our thinking enables us to rationalise, to discriminate between good and bad, to have a dialogue between our higher consciousness, our Spirit, and our lower consciousness, our Ego. But in addition, many of us will also hear voices outside of the normal perimeter of our thinking. These extra-terrestrial voices, as I call them, can be experienced by anyone from any walk of life no matter what their social standing or educational and intellectual achievements might be, or lack thereof. I have met many people, male and female of all ages, who have told me about their experiences of hearing voices outside of their own thinking, very often voices accompanied with the mental image of a loved one passed over. This is not an uncommon experience and can continue to happen years after the loved one has passed on.

Mary, who was a play-ground monitor at a local junior school whose husband died suddenly of a heart attack while still in his fifties. Mary still communicated with him years later, because she said, he was always passing on good advice. She said his voice was always accompanied with a strong sensation that he was close. Despite his physical demise, Mary was convinced her husband was always looking out for her in his usual caring manner. As he did in life, so he did in death. Another example is when close friends of our family lost their only child, a seventeen-year-old son in a car accident. The husband who had always held down managerial positions within the aviation industry would have considered himself very down to earth, practical, and rational thinking. Yet in the years that followed their son's passing, this man was not only convinced his son's energy remained in the house, but from time to time, he would hear his son's voice speaking to him. He used to tell me that he felt his son was just as close in death as he used to be in life. Again, a psychiatrist might conclude that grief can give rise to such imaginations, a sort of safety net, helping us to adjust to a situation we would rather not face up to. And yet more than 30 years later, the grief this man and his wife experienced has dissipated as they have travelled down a different road encouraged by the voice of their deceased son to take other turnings in life. Following their son's advice, they became foster parents to children who were mentally and physically challenged establishing emotional fulfilment for all concerned.

I have known children who speak or play with "special" friends that no one else can hear or see. These children have heard their invisible friends speaking to them. Years ago, before the advance of technology, children were invited into a world of so-called imagination in which to amuse themselves. Children could get lost in a world of pretend. My own sister was always lost in such a world. Sometimes I used to catch glimpses of bright lights dancing around her. There was no form to these bright lights, yet I knew intuitively they were connected to the Angel Realm. Around my sister there was always a sense of peaceful equilibrium as she became engrossed with her pretend play born of her imagination. So, when we talk about imagination, what do we mean? Collins dictionary on-line explains imagination as "the ability that you have to form pictures or ideas in your mind of things that are new and exciting that you have not experienced."[3] In other words, our imagination is conjured up by our rational thinking self, freeing us from the world we're in to be in a world somewhere else. Many people might think imagination is a figment of its own making, but according to my Spiritual messages, images that come to us via our imagination have come directly from the Universal Spirit or other energies around us, and far from being unreal or unrealistic, imagination affords us access into infinite parallel realities. Thus, imagination is the faculty that facilitates our communication ability to other energies around us enabling the source to positive and/or negative ideas or notions depending on the energies in which we have linked into. Imagination can be the vehicle in which inspiration and aspiration and visionary creative concepts come to us, via universal energies of those that have gone before us and from the infinite cosmos. Equally, the opposite can be conceived when we become partners to destructive negative energies and all that this entails. Thus, when we use our imagination, it can be described as utilising information linked into a two-way radio. One airway station transmits positivity and creativity born of Spirit, our higher consciousness. The other airway station transmits negativity and destruction born of Ego, our lower consciousness.

As children, we are hugely sensitive to the hidden energies around us that are directly linked into the universal energies. Some children are supersensitive, others just generally so to the undercurrents of the world. Huge responsibility thus lies with how children are brought up and the environments in which they live. Children's innate sensitivity warrants they absorb positive or negative energies like little sponges. Cultural and social conditioning along with parental role models can eventually dilute, erode, or destroy this wonderful attribute of sensitivity. Responsibility thus lies with society and parents and adult role models to make sure the sensitivities of children are retained and amplified, encouraging development of their psychic faculty and imagination for the betterment of themselves and the world they live in. A child's sensitivity, their psychic and telepathic attributes, are a channel to imagination and therefore important to the future of the planet and generations that follow. My own grandson Liam, who is hugely sensitive and psychic, has described seeing multiple people, and even a loved pet rabbit, that no one else could see or hear. One entity was a man who was thought to be a previous owner to the house they were living in at the time, long since passed away. Liam's father, my son has told me that none of Liam's experiences could be explained in the context of imaginative play, and some were in fact quite distressing. (Interestingly, the scary entities could be "sent away" with a firm instruction to leave him alone!) This type of event is not uncommon where children are concerned. A young child has not been living long enough to have had his psychic sensitivities eroded too much, allowing them to tap into the hidden energies around them. The experience of hearing voices in our head in some cases accompanied with visitations, can happen any time of day or night at any age. Thus, to suggest to a parent that their child is psychologically disturbed is hugely damaging for both parties. If society continues to dismantle the Truth which is conveyed to us through our innate sensitivity, along with suggesting that imagination bears no substance to reality, it is in danger of eroding the psychic and telepathic ability which is born to every man, woman, and child.

Every second of the day and night our brain and mind are alive and working. During the day, we think. During the night, we dream. Visitations and communication from deceased loved ones can often come via our dreams. The voices we hear inside our head via our dreams are real. We know the brain can be surgically removed. We can find pictures of it on websites or in books, many of us will know what a human brain looks like. But where is the mind and where does our thinking come from? Man creates his own environment through his thought processes. But where do his thoughts and/or ideas come from? Again, we might conclude that our faculty of imagination, our creative attribute plays a huge role in this process. But are we also for the most part without realising it linked in telepathically to other universal information? When we physically die, we know that our brain also perishes. It decomposes like the rest of our physical body. But what about our thinking and mental faculty? Does the energy and the memory thereof dissipate into the ethos where it still communicates as an entity without form? We know scientifically and medically, without the brain working, without the mind, there is no "us" despite times when the body is still functioning. So, we should conclude, the mind is who we are. Here I am reminded of the French philosopher René Descartes {1596/1650} who built his philosophy on the premise which he held to be indisputable and that was, the existence of himself as a thinking subject.

"Cogito ergo sum".
"I think therefore I am".

In the modern World, it is now not uncommon to believe that once you are dead, you are dead. The idea of having a Spirit or Soul has now become a laughing matter. So, what do we mean by Spirit or Soul? Again, I refer to the Collins dictionary on-line which writes "your soul/spirit is the part of you that consists of your mind, character, thoughts and feelings. It is the nonphysical part of you that is believed to remain alive after physical death."[3] So if we accept the premise that within each of us exists a Soul or Spirit then we need to ask, where does it reside within our body? Descartes argued that the Soul/Spirit was the rational thinking part of the mind which interacted with the body through the pineal gland. This tiny cone-shaped organ is located behind and above the pituitary gland almost directly in the middle of the brain and has become known in many esoteric schools of thought as the "Third Eye". In his book "DMT The Spirit Module" Dr Rick Straussman {February 8, 1952/ } hypothesises that a powerful entheogen, which he refers to as the "God module" or "Spirit module" is produced in the pineal gland creating the ability to contact those outside of the living human realm. [4] On the other hand, Steve Taylor argues, that a Spirit Force pervades the universe and manifests itself in two ways. First that matter is the external manifestation, while mind in complex forms of matter is the internal manifestation of Spirit.[5]

From my own experiences of Spiritual mediumship and hearing voices as separate entities from my thinking self, it is now my theory that because our mind is without corporeal substance and form, our mental thinking faculty, which incorporates psychic knowledge, has the capacity to live on through space and time after our physical demise. From this standpoint, we may conclude our mind contains our Spirit or Soul; it's one and the same, our higher consciousness. But the mind also contains our Ego, our lower consciousness. Thus, if we take the premise that the existence of Spirit and Ego relies on our thinking/mental faculty which is contained within our brain, we need to ask: where does our thinking faculty get its information from? We may argue that secular cultural information is learnt from birth to old age. However, very often, we seem to know things without knowing how we have come to know them. Is this inherited knowledge that is passed on from generation to generation through our DNA? My theory is that this psychic knowledge can exist beyond time and space and is communicated telepathically while living in the profane world, but also after our physical demise.

I have found over my lifetime I am telepathically connected to my children, people I love dearly and even particular friends and pets. Years ago, I had a very close friend. She was always arriving on my doorstep just when I was thinking about her. We used to joke that we would save a lot of money on telephone bills if we simply relied on telepathic communication. We were somehow always on the same wavelength. We are all born to a lesser or greater extent with telepathic ability which is all part of our psychic attributes. And far from being a sign of mental disorientation or disease, hearing voices in our head is the faculty of superior, infinite communicative intelligence. It is the making of Clairaudience, the faculty of a Medium in touch with the Spiritual Realm and all other energies around them. It is the gift from the Divine Universal energy of our Creator given to all sentient creatures enabling them to tune into the energies of their environment. Spirit finds many ways to contact us through a voice in our head, such as in an auditory impression in a piece of music, a song, or just dropping a subtle message through telepathic communication. It is about our rational conscious mind correlating with our psychic subconscious telepathically linked into the universal energies that go beyond the place and times we live in. These omnipresent, omnipotent, and omniscient universal energies can be full of abundant wisdom and knowledge. Equally, they can be full of destructive urges. Thus, it could be argued these external voices could be explained as coming in from a cosmic universal telephone exchange. An infinite cosmic network of information, either born of higher entities and those that have gone before us, departing wisdom for the betterment of the world. Or destructive urges born of Hades.

The website “Hearing Voices Network" described several different theories and ideas as to why some people hear voices or experience visitations. Some theories put forward suggest it may involve having a special gift or sensitivity following adverse experiences or traumatic events. Or it may involve biochemical imbalances or emotional/physical health disparities, cognitive error or simply setting oneself up as somehow special from the rest of humanity. When properly assessed, we learn that hearing voices outside of our usual thinking is not so uncommon. In fact, many people testify to hearing voices which has also been accompanied with a vision, a smell, a taste, a feeling, or a touch or even a knocking or scratching sound. For the most part, these experiences are fleeting, but social conditioning warrants instant dismissal urging many people to seek some rational explanation. Embarrassment or fear of being labelled an idiot with an acute imagination, or worse, having a mental illness, leaves many people hiding their experiences. Yet, they are far from alone. Many famous and important people down through the ages have contributed greatly to human creativity. For example, Charles Dickens contributed greatly to our understanding of the human condition. It is said he became so involved with his characters, he believed they spoke to him. While Robert Schumann {1810/1856} a German composer and pianist composed beautiful romantic music under the urge of inner voices that both plagued and blessed him throughout his life. It is said, that while his mind remained organised, he felt in control with what he heard from his voices, and he produced some of his finest works. But sometimes his inner voices changed from angelic helpers to tormentors of the underworld. [6] There are many accounts within Christianity, Islam, and Judaism where the voice of God or the Angels are found addressing humans in speech, calling them to account, entering dialogue, listening to their concerns, and answering their questions. Doris Stokes, the renowned English Spiritual Medium is said to have always understood her experiences of the paranormal as being extremely Spiritual. And Socrates considered the voice inside his head as a form of "Divine madness" daemonic in its independence, which he only heard when he was about to make a mistake. Socrates viewed his voice as a gift from the gods which saved him from entering politics and encouraged him instead into poetry, creativity, mysticism, love and philosophy. While St John the Cross, a 16th century Spanish theologian and catholic priest recognised three types of voices that he heard. He argued there were voices that saved which came to people when they were in danger or under stress or undergoing some physical threat. And there were voices which gave novel and creative information. But more importantly, there was the voice within our self that is directly linked to the Spiritual realm. According to St John, all three types of voices are supernatural communications which can be accessed through silence, contemplation, prayer, and meditation. [6]

Joan of Arc was only a young teenager when she first became conscious of hearing voices outside of her normal thinking. She called these voices her counsel which apparently came to her in a blaze of light which she recognised as Angels. At first, she had been reluctant to speak of her voices. But when it eventually became known, she was labelled mad or an impostor or a liar and eventually to her detriment, she was labelled a sorceress for which she was burnt at the stake. Yet this simple farm girl at the age of nineteen, following the instructions of her voices, executed what was to become known as a brilliant military and political masterpiece that saved France. Mahatma Gandhi gave credit of his actions to the voice within him which he followed with unwavering conviction all through his life as the voice of God. Dismissing imagination, hallucination and dreaming, Gandhi stood firm in his belief that he was listening to the voice of God right up to the end of his life. Using weapons of passive resistance and determination, conscience and truth,

Gandhi and his followers fought and won India's independence.[6] While in more recent times, the Irish Mystic, Lorna Byrne claims to hear and see Angels transcribes the messages from the Angels in her books giving comfort, inspiration, courage, and hope to millions of people around the world [7]

My Guardian Angels and Spirit guide have changed over my lifetime in accordance with psychological, emotional, and Spiritual growth. It is about having guidance as we journey through life. My first Spirit Guide was my great grandmother, Mary Anne Cheek. This was followed by her son, my grandad. In more recent years it is been my brother, sometimes my dad and sometimes my great aunts Mary and Grace who now give me guidance in mediumship development. Sometimes we may hear great wisdom being passed on to us from some higher being. We may not know who this higher being is, but the experience is tremendously joyful and enlightening leading to inspiration and creativity. Other times we may hear words of great comfort at a time when it is most needed. Sometimes we may hear things we prefer not to hear leaving feelings of distress or foreboding. Sometimes the voice might turn us away from things we should not be doing. Or we may become a stool pigeon or handmaiden to energies of the underworld repeating human atrocities that have gone before. Either way, the ability to "hear" and sometimes experience visitations, smells, touch, or sounds relies on the human make-up of our psychic faculty, a faculty of intuition, psychic vision, psychic hearing, and telepathy that I believe is innate to all sentient creatures. It is now my theory that the human mind's ability to rationalise has developed over time, but it still retains its basic instincts, the psychic faculty that helps us telepathically to stay linked into the universal energies around us and above us, acting as if a satellite dish, enabling vast communication from all directions travelling over time and space. Science is still in its infancy and in accordance with

Descartes' pursuit of wisdom, science has a long way to go before it unveils the Truth involving the workings of the Mind and the Voice who visits from time to time.

Chapter 2

Life and Death

Mistakenly, many people presume that a Spiritual Medium is a person that must be overly concerned with death or contacting the dead, and that there must be a morbid curiosity with the notion of "another world". However, that is not the case. Like all human beings on planet Earth, I consider myself to be normal and well-balanced going about ordinary mundane activities in my daily life. If I can claim I am different in any way, and I am not making that claim, it's because sometimes, when it seems appropriate to do so, "the other side" will contact me with information. Information that I can convey to the world at large through my books, or information I can convey to individuals that come for a private consultation. The idea that mediumship is merely a parlour game, or a circus act is far from the truth, although sadly such charlatans and scams have existed for as long as human history. Cynicism and scepticism are born of fear, and a closed mind which is born of the Ego. But a Spiritual Medium is open to Spirit thus can be classified as a messenger that works with and for the Spiritual realm, the Angels and ultimately God. As a messenger that conveys messages of hope, friendship and love, people come to realise that they are not alone, that their loved ones who have passed on are not far away or no longer in pain and suffering, and that death is not to be feared nor is it the end. It could be said that mediumship brings healing. And so, when people say to me,

"If you're in touch with the other side, how come they don't tell you things like the lottery numbers?"

I gently tell them, I am not a fortune teller, and that I have learnt over the years the information conveyed to me via the Spiritual realm is considered more important than material wealth. At this point in my life, now in my seventies, I have learnt we are all on a different life journey. And if it is our destiny or fate to be rich or famous no matter what road we come by it, then before we end our life here on Earth, we will achieve what we are destined to achieve (along with the life lessons thereof!). As a human being above all else, I am still very much exposed to all the mundane challenges in my daily life that other human beings are also exposed to. I have my positive and negative attributes like everyone else in dealing with these challenges, and consequently my life has not always turned out the way I would have liked. So, as I have grown older, Spiritual wisdom has developed as I have learnt my life lessons. Now I can see a thread in life that connects us to the concept of death. There is no death as we interpret it, only an energy that goes on, because energy is what we are in life, and so it continues. It is our Life Force, the very essence of who we are. All things on planet Earth, both animate and inanimate, extol energy. The universe is energy, as science now demonstrates – Einstein's famous equation $E=mc^2$ proves the link between energy and matter itself! We become aware of unseen energy when we use our utilities of gas or electricity. We should consider electro-magnetic energy in the same manner. There are many ways in which electro-magnetic energy is in use in the modern world such as radio waves, rays, radar, and other means of communication. Somewhere in the back of my mind I also remember that colour exudes energy as it has recently been discovered with the growing of plants in specialised garden nurseries and viruses in scientific laboratories, although this would have to be verified. Being a Spiritual Medium is not about a person who has a morbid curiosity for the dead, but it is a person who is highly sensitive with heightened psychic ability to tune into this "energy" of life no matter what form it takes, and within this form of energy lies the memory of the life thereof. Consider it a memory bank, a store full of information that a highly gifted Spiritual Medium can tune into. Thus, being a Spiritual Medium not only equips us to tune into the "essence" of life passed on, but also equips us to tune into the "essence" of life still living in this world.

My brother who has passed on, having shortened his own life through alcohol addiction, often pays me a "visit" during times when I feel down or out of sorts. At these times, my whole being becomes goose-bumped and consumed in a bright light not of this world. With his image in my mind's eye, he speaks a message which is always the same,

> "Life is for joy and for living Sis"
> "Joy can be found in helping others".
> "Joy can be found in the simple pleasures of life".
> "Joy is in the miracle of life no matter what form it takes."
> "Life is precious".

Since my brother's passing, I have been more convinced of the value of life and the joy of living, enjoying life in simple ways. But sadly, in the modern developed world much emphasis is placed on material wealth and satisfying one's own Ego, which is why the world is in such a mess. We all know about climate change for example, but we all continue to use fossil fuels to warm our homes and drive our industries or fuel our cars or fly around the world on foreign holidays. We convince ourselves we care, but none of us are prepared to change our ways or compromise enough to make much difference to the environment and other life on planet Earth. Watching images of war, conflict, violence and suffering on our televisions in the comfort of our homes ensures a sense of detachment: it is not our problem, it's someone else's! We give to charity to alleviate some of our guilt, but we do want the problem on our doorstep. Some people become desensitised and have trouble distinguishing between what is real and what is entertainment. For many people around the world, life is not full of joy, but a constant battle for survival pitted with financial hardship, worry and fear. For many people around the world, life is scarred with illness, or disease, or disability. For many people around the world, life is scarred with abuse, or criminality, or war and conflict. For many people around the world, life is scarred with poverty and struggle. For some people, there is a longing for death to bring about release from pain or worry. Depression urges suicide. Illness or pain urges euthanasia. The messages I receive these days from the "other side" now convey a sense of urgency on more worldly matters. I am informed that the world is at a crossroads. We have a choice of two directions. The path of Love and Light born out of sharing, caring, tolerance and compassion for all life on planet Earth, where we use our intelligence to empathise with Life for a kinder, more eco-friendly planet. Or the path of Hate and Darkness born out of greed, selfishness, indifference, and intolerance, leading to war and conflict and destruction. Thus, Spirit and Ego fight for supremacy.

In society the subject of death is rarely discussed privately or in the public arena. Generally, people will ignore discussing the subject or facing up to its existence, and yet it is with us all the time running parallel to life. In youth, death seems a long way off and has nothing to do with us. Death is perceived to only happen to the aged or the sick or is visited upon us by accident. Youthful ignorance and arrogance ignore the fact, that death can come knocking at anyone's door at any time. Death comes calling for all sentient Life and vegetation releasing its energy into a universal ether, a Spiritual realm which we call home, and where the Angels and God reside. Without death, there cannot be rebirth. As a Spiritual Medium, I am utterly convinced that all animal species, including that of Homo sapiens, are connected by the same great universal energy, and thus deserves the same considerations. Having the ability to read the aura of all species convinces me of this. Many years ago, when I worked as a technical tracer at Westland aircraft factory in Yeovil Somerset, one day the draughtsman sitting behind me said,

"Carol, if you put as much energy into human care as you do with animals, I might be able to admire you!"

My working colleague was not and is not unusual in this attitude. This man's disparaging remark was made to undermine my great love of animals and my conviction that all life deserves equal consideration. He made the comment just after my very old much-loved pet cat Fuzzy had passed on. Despite months of care and many visits to the vet, the cancer she suffered from was to eventually claim her. It was her time to go. Many people would regard energies devoted to the welfare and care of animals as being worthless. For me this has never been the case. For me, caring for other species equates to the same care and consideration as I would donate to humankind. In Ireland, on my walks out into the country lanes, it saddens me to see horses or donkeys stood alone in a field without access to shelter or water. The fields they are standing in are very often waterlogged and worthless in their nourishment. I can observe from their aura that these animals feel alone which in turn heightens their sense of fear. I can observe from their body language that they feel downhearted. In bad winter weather, not only are they devoid of decent grass to eat, but also nourishment of extra food and fresh hay and companionship. Horses and donkeys are herd animals, they need social interaction of their own kind. They are also fiercely loyal animals to deserving owners. Putting them in a field on their own for months on end without contact with their own kind and/or human companionship is not only neglectful, but in my opinion, is deeply cruel. The same can be said for any animal that belongs in its natural indigenous state within a herd. Of course, many people would be appalled if they were labelled cruel in their treatment of animals. For them, treatment of animals and treatment of human beings are two entirely different considerations. And yet it might be worth considering a quote by Gandhi who said,

"The greatness of a nation and its moral progress can be judged by the way its animals are treated. I hold that the more helpless a creature the more entitled it is to protection by man from the cruelty of humankind.

Gandhi's quote is loaded in its considerations not least to underwrite the notion that all species are equally deserving of compassion. And if equality took precedence in our considerations towards other species, the human species might not be so barbaric and indifferent to its own kind. It is about having respect for Life and knowing that All Life on planet Earth is worth the same considerations. If we could go down that road, perhaps conditions of poverty, homelessness, war, conflict, violence, intimidation and abuse, and the extinction of other species and the consequences to the planet and the suffering thereof could be eliminated, bringing joy to the Soul and Spirit of all living things.

When our much-loved schnauzer Myfanwy passed-on, it was a shock, not just to us, but our much-loved Labrador Megan and our little Jack Russell Sophie. Myfanwy had passed-away suddenly after a heart attack following an epileptic fit, a condition she had suffered from all her life. I could observe from Megan's and Sophie's body language they were feeling downhearted as they entered a period of adjustment after losing a dear companion. Although not off their food, they appeared a little lost for a while as if adjusting to their new pecking order in the pack which was now smaller. A few years later, at the age of seventeen, Megan also passed-away leaving Sophie on her own for the first time in her life. What had been a period of adjustment when Myfanwy passed on now turned into a consuming grief. In the weeks and months following Megan's passing, Sophie was completely off her food spending time alone in her little bed brooding, no longer "asking" for her walks. Observation of her body language informed me she had entered a period of dark melancholy. Nothing seemed to provoke her out of this state of obvious bereavement not even a tasty morsel of a piece of chicken from my husband's plate! Sophie had shrunk into herself, isolating herself from life. This situation continued into the summer until our grandchildren from the UK and America arrived on a visit. Taking Sophie up into the back garden for a game of football, our grandchildren unwittingly brought Sophie out of herself. They had given this little dog a reason to enjoy life again. Three years later, my husband and I noticed lumps appearing on Sophie's tummy. A visit to the vets confirmed she had mammary cancer. The operation which followed was a success, but only bought our little dog an extra seven months of life. We had been warned the cancer might spread to other vital organs and by the spring of the following year, it had. Sophie was on painkillers for a while, but these only masked the pain she was in. An x-ray confirmed the cancer was aggressive and rampant. The spark within her which had been reignited by our grandchildren was still there despite the pain which enabled her to wag her tail in our presence. Nevertheless, we knew the decision we had to make was going to be painful, but not as painful as it would be for Sophie if she continued living.

Selfishly, I cancelled the first arranged date when our vet was to come to the house. I could not bear the thought of losing yet another doggy companion and the last of a bunch of doggy companions over the last twenty-three years. One day, as Sophie lay in her bed, I was kneeling beside her asking the Spiritual realm for healing energy, help and guidance. I suddenly became aware of my dad's presence. My darling father had passed-away some twelve years previously and he often makes himself known to me when I'm upset or worried. During these times, as always, my skin becomes covered in goose bumps and I feel a great sense that someone is close, while at the same time, I receive a mental picture in my mind's eye of who is "visiting". On this occasion I heard my dad say,

"It is time to let Sophie go Love".
"She is a loyal little dog, and only stays because of you".
"It is now Sophie's time to go, and it is up to you to help her".

Dad's message left me in no doubt that no matter how unpleasant our task might be, it was time to let Sophie go. Sophie was riddled with cancer. She was in great pain. We knew her days were numbered. We could not allow her to go on any longer in this state of suffering. The following day, we called our vet to the house once again, and while Sophie was cradled in my arms, he put our dear doggy companion to sleep. My experience of keeping animals, especially dogs and seeing their reaction to losing one of their own companions leaves me in no doubt that other animal species also experience a sense of loss and bereavement. I daresay many other pet owners could vouch to similar circumstances. Keeping a pet or looking after other animals reminds us that we are not so dissimilar in our requirements and feelings. Looking after other species reminds us that all life is special and deserves the same considerations. It is not easy for those of us who believe in the sanctity of Life. And with all that modern science and technology can now provide it is hard to let go when life is threatened with age and disease. It is tempting to prolong life, if possible, when science and medicine provides the means to do so especially when it comes to human life. And yet, when our pet becomes ill, we call in the vet to "still" the agony – ironically, we are not usually so kind to our fellow humans! Perhaps this is because of our lack of understanding of Life and Death and the continuation of the Soul, Spiritual energy of the being.

During her treatment for leukaemia, there were many times when my auntie Margaret found it all too much. My dad's eldest sister was a much-loved lady in her seventies when she was diagnosed with this debilitating disease. This lovely kind-hearted genteel lady was amid retirement, enjoying her friendships, her church and her hobby of painting when her life and the life of her family was turned upside down. It was hard for her to cope psychologically and physically, but it was equally hard for her family to cope emotionally. Bearing witness to the slow death of someone you love is heart breaking. The urge to prolong life is strong. I received a phone call early one evening, it was auntie Margaret. She sounded extremely tired and was very tearful. Having spent the whole day as an outpatient in hospital waiting to receive her chemotherapy treatment, she was now exhausted.

"I can't go on" she told me between sobbing.

Auntie Margaret went on to tell me that she had spent all morning in a hot noisy hospital corridor waiting for her treatment. The staff were caring but had been run off their feet. Mostly she had been ignored. And when she did eventually receive her treatment, she found it uncomfortable and nauseating. She confided in me that she wanted to give up her treatment because she was ready to go.

"This is no way to live" she said.
"I am ready to be with my maker".
The trouble is the children don't want me to go".
"They want me to keep fighting on".

I explained to auntie Margaret that the family loved her very much and it is hard for all of us, especially my cousins, her children, to come to terms with what is taking place. I told her it is not easy for them to let her go and that loving someone can sometimes blind us to what is best for them. Having converted to Catholicism when she married Uncle Bernard, auntie Margaret's religion and her faith were very important to her and gave her inner strength when physical strength failed her.

"Ask God and the Angels to support you" I told her.
"This will give you the strength you need until God calls you".
"You will know instinctively when your time has come".

I told her that I loved her very much and so does her family. She is to hang onto that. Auntie Margaret was to live a further month or so. She spent some of this time visiting family in the south-west of England. Having reconnected emotionally with people she loved, a sudden feeling of urgency overwhelmed her, urging her to ask her son Roger to drive quickly back to the North. The North of England had been her adopted homeland and where she was now receiving hospice care. Instinct had informed auntie Margaret her time was near. She passed over with her family around her the morning after her return.

On the passing of a beloved pet, I have often been asked by a client,

"Will I see my pet again?"
"Does my pet have a Spirit?"
"Does my pet have a Soul?"

I can only answer in accordance with my own experiences. I can tell you about the time when I was walking alone along the beach soon after our dear little Jack Russell Sophie had been put to sleep. The spring sun was shining brightly against a beautiful blue sky and the tide had gone out to Boston leaving Lahinch beach massive and deserted, only scattered with a few doggie walking people. Suddenly, without warning, my heavy heart was lifted by sheer joy that hit my solar plexus. There before me, I could "see" in my mind's eye, Myfanwy, and Megan with Banjo now also passed-over our son's Lurcher who had stayed with us briefly for eighteen months while Daniel was in Australia, all prancing and chasing each other around at my feet as doggies do when winding each other up in play, out on a walk across the beach. Sophie was there amongst the others barking in excitement. Their Spiritual body language conveyed to me, our doggy friends were all right, they were together, they were having fun, they were well again.

In answer to my client's question, I can say categorically,

"Yes, you will"
"And yes, they do".

Death comes to us all no matter what lifeform we are in. Death waits for no Man or other lifeforms. We are all in the same queue. Life links us to death and death links us to Life, a Life beyond our physical demise. There is a time to live an earthly life. And there is a time to pass-on and go "home". My own experiences of Spirit and of the Spiritual Realm have conveyed to me the firm belief that no matter what lifeform we are in, all life has a Spirit which is linked into a greater Universal Spirit conveying a Spiritual Truth.

These experiences informed me of profound truths. The first was, that all sentient animals experience and suffer the same emotions, emotions of attachment, fear, joy, loss, or bereavement. The second truth is, that we all have a "time" when life as we know it must come to an end. And no matter how hard we try to prolong life, an ending in the physical sense is inevitable. Very often, this urge to prolong life is born out of selfish considerations. We cannot bear the thought of losing someone dear to us. We cannot bear the thought of having to say goodbye. Even I, as a Spiritual Medium allowed my human attributes to take over because I hated the thought of losing yet another dear doggy companion. There is also sometimes the fear of death itself, the unknown and the unknowing. And yet, I can tell you without hesitation, there is another Life after this one. And death itself is not the ultimate end, but with the demise of our physical self, releases us into another realm. And our loved ones who have passed-on before us are there to welcome us "home". We have no reason to suppose in this life that they are not listening in and that they are ready to speak to us whenever we wish to speak to them. Death is thus not the end, but only another beginning.

In recent times, I have been informed by my brother, who now resides on the "other side" that in the moment of our passing, we feel no pain or fear. In the moment of our last breath, our Spirit is simply released from our physical body, and we are free to go at will. Family and/or friendships are always there to greet us, even those that perhaps in life, we have had a falling out with. In our next life, it is time to put past hurts and grievances behind us. Only Love and Forgiveness prevail. I have been informed by my brother, that the moment we pass-over, we realise our past mistakes and experience misgivings. The moment we pass-over, a bright light prevails highlighting all the things that were wrong in our earthly life. He says, it is like having a blindfold removed from our eyes. Suddenly, we see things much clearer. At that point, we are preparing for another Life. Preparation for this new Life is through tutoring by celestial beings until such time it is thought we are ready to enter another life again here on earth. For some people, they will not return to earth as they have aspired and obtained great Spiritual insight and wisdom. The Law of Cause and Effect no longer concerns them. Thus, in this life here on earth, as individuals, we are each at a different Spiritual level in accordance with our Spiritual development and attainment. This makes us all unique from each other as we each view life from different angles and perspectives. And in accordance with our earthly experiences, we will each have a different worldview.

Some years ago, during a telephone conversation with my son Daniel, he made a disparaging remark about my brother Nigel. I was attempting to explain to Daniel, who did not believe in the concept of Spiritual mediumship at this time that I had received messages from my brother. Daniel drew in his breath with impatience on my topic of conversation.

"Mum, it is hard to believe that Nigel could have the aptitude to pass on any good advice, given that he was an alcoholic!"

This is a common reaction from anyone, whether related or not. The subjects of Spiritual mediumship and/or psychic phenomena are often used as the butt for rude remarks or crude jokes. Over the years, age and maturity have enabled me with patience to deal with such ignorance with impunity and grace.

"On the contrary, Daniel."
"Recognising one's own weaknesses and recognising one has made mistakes,
surely ensures one is more able to pass on good advice?"

Making mistakes in this life does not make us a bad person. Mistakes are learning curves; they help us to develop into better people. By learning through our mistakes, we are tapping into and utilising our higher consciousness our Spirit within. People who appear to be oozing evil, those that carry out dreadful acts of barbarism are also on a learning curve. But their journey is longer as they tap into and utilise their lower consciousness the Ego. In traditional religious terms, it is known as the Devil. The Ego can be selfish, greedy, self-centred, inconsiderate, intolerant, egotistical, intimidating, uncaring, unloving, indifferent and/or violent and aggressive as it pushes hard to meet its own agenda. The problems and the troubles that challenge the modern world are an outcome of the Ego centred human population. Spirit works for the Light. Ego works for Darkness. All our experiences will shape and mould us. At the end of our earthly life, we will each be the sum-total of all our thoughts and actions.

Chapter 3

Spirit or ghost?

Every time I went upstairs, the door to the bathroom and the door to the spare bedroom had been closed. The first couple of times it happened I simply opened these doors again. Since the installation of a rather overly efficient wood burner in the sitting room downstairs, my husband and I had started to make sure that the rooms upstairs also enjoyed the circulating warm air. But our determination to be more efficient in our old tiny modest cottage seemed not to be taking place. I kept thinking to myself, am I losing my marbles? Perhaps I'm getting forgetful in my old age and simple thought I had opened the doors? However, by mid-afternoon, having found the doors closed once again, I was becoming very puzzled and quite irritable over the matter. Believing that my husband was closing the doors after I had opened them, I called downstairs to him as he sat in the sitting room,

"Derm, why do you keep closing the doors upstairs?"
"I thought we wanted the whole house to feel the benefit of the warm air?"

There was silence for a minute or two before my husband appeared at the bottom of the stairs.

"What are you talking about?" he called.
"I haven't been closing any doors."

This door episode continued periodically throughout the week leaving both my husband and I totally flummoxed. Sunday came and later in the evening I received my usual phone call from Becky, my daughter. My husband and I now live on the west coast of Southern Ireland while Becky was still living in the city of Bristol in the UK. We usually tried to catch up at the end of each week. While exchanging news and opinions on what had transpired in her life over the last seven days, Becky suddenly announced,

"Oh yes, I also went to see my friend Claire."

"Tell me mum, have you had any odd experiences in your life recently?"

"Why do you ask" I said?

Becky had often spoken of her friend Claire who like me was a psychic and Spiritual Medium. In recent times, she had apparently gone public and often practised on her friends. Becky had said she was very good. On one occasion, when Becky had lived in Bath, Claire had utterly gobsmacked her by telling her to start wearing her helmet when out riding her bike in the city. Becky asked her,

"How on earth do you know I haven't been wearing my helmet?"

Claire told her that an old man called Donald is always with her and is worried about her safety. Claire said,

"He is telling me to tell you to take more care."

Unbeknown to Claire, Becky's deceased grandfather, my dad was called Donald! Now in more recent times, Becky had only been in the room a few minutes when Claire was to tell her that her mum was rather upset due to circumstances surrounding her, but not to worry, it's a storm in a teacup. Claire went on to tell Becky she was receiving her information from her mum's younger brother who was now deceased but is always with her, and to remind her of this, he had recently been playing tricks on her. He had been opening and closing doors! Once again, Becky was gobsmacked at this information because she had never discussed with her friend Claire the fact that her mother had a deceased brother.

As a Spiritual Medium, I am always on the other end of the spectrum passing on information to my own clients. But this was a new experience for me. I have never met Claire, nor had I divulged to Becky in our conversation that I had indeed been upset all week. In fact, unbeknown to Becky, or anyone else outside of our home, the old man who lived next door had been in one of his cantankerous moods and subjected my husband and me to rather nasty comments during the week. It was not the first time it had happened and as on other occasions, his insults had induced a longing for improved finances, so we could purchase our own home once more. His rude comments always serve to remind me of our vulnerable financial position and the things we must put up with just to keep a roof over our heads! However, my brother's spiritual message from the "other side" did serve to remind me that so often, life situations we regard as serious are no more than "storms in a teacup" and not worth a reaction!

Like a lot of little boys, when my brother was a child, he was always up to something that perhaps he should not be up to. One of his greatest kicks was to get our dad to take him to the joke shop in Yeovil where he loved to spend his pocket money. He loved anything that induced the element of surprise on some poor unsuspecting recipient, usually his elder sister! I was very often the butt of one of his jokes or tricks. Over time I got used to it and always played up to the moment, pretending to be cross on the one hand but quietly sniggering to myself on the other. Acting as if I was about to give chase, Nigel would run ahead shouting over a shoulder,

"Don't worry Sis".
"I'm just playing tricks on you".

My brother is the only person in my life that has ever used that phrase, "I'm just playing tricks on you". Those words given to me again by Becky's friend Claire have brought the greatest comfort of all and serve to remind me that the small irritations in this world are of little consequence compared to the greater picture. If I ever needed proof that the Spirit does indeed live on, then this episode of closed doors must surely be one of those most profound experiences of an afterlife. Another such experience also involves intervention from the Spiritual realm. In recent years, whenever my husband and I have exchanged crosswords, we have noticed that many of the family photos hanging from the walls become tilted at an odd angle including an oil painting of a family gathering on Lahinch beach and a pencil etching of my husband and me by a pavement artist in Paris when we were on honeymoon. We have never witnessed any of these pictures being moved. Yet coming down in the morning, the day after an argument, we can be sure that everything hanging on the wall to do with the family will be hanging at an odd angle. It's as if our attention is being drawn to the importance of our relationship and the unity of our own family. These experiences of intervention from the Spirit world serve to remind me of the danger of becoming enmeshed in petty squabbles and worries born out of fear, pride, pig-headedness, or unreasonableness. These strange experiences always leave me feeling ashamed thus uncomfortable because I know in my heart that my behaviour has been "witnessed" by another like the time my deceased grandfather told me off when I was a child for playing around in a public loo. I know in my heart, that the Spirit World in its own way is attempting to teach me lessons, lessons about myself and the world at large. Intervention from the Spirit World remind me that the route to living in peace and harmony rests on the virtues of tolerance, patience, and compromise. Now, instead of feeling sorry for myself and playing the role of a victim I try desperately hard to empower myself by sending prayers and compassion out to the source of irritation. We must always try to stand back from the source of irritation and ask why? Take a deep breath and try to look compassionately and harmoniously at the situation and all those people involved including oneself. Intervention from the Spirit World brings comfort in showing us its existence while at the same time, teaching us valuable lessons on how to live more peacefully in this life thus bringing contentment and joy.

In the years leading up to my mother-in-law's passing, her once a week telephone calls suddenly increased in number. We started hearing from her more than once during the day or in the early evenings. We knew she must be worried about something given that she would not usually make too many long-distance phone calls from the UK to Ireland in one week. She had lived in the same house for sixty years but had been widowed for thirty years, living a very happy active healthy life over that time. Usually she was a very contented gentle lady, but suddenly her phone calls began to reveal someone who was becoming increasingly irritable and nervous. Following one such phone call, I asked her if there was anything bothering her? Only when pressed did she confide in me that she now hated sitting in the house on her own. She told me that her little dining room now looked like a doctor's waiting room. This was because she could "see" members of her deceased family sitting there as if waiting for her to join them. She told me she had started to "see" and "feel" the presence of her deceased husband who she said was following her about the house. In all the years of widowhood she told me, she had never had visitations from her deceased husband before. Quite naturally these experiences were upsetting and unnerving her. Her conversations on the phone left us in no doubt that she should spend more time with her family, particularly her son, my husband whom she was very close to. Eager to induce a little more happiness into her life we invited her to stay with us here in Ireland for a little while. During her two-month stay, mum was continually reminiscing about her past life, especially her childhood in the North of Ireland. It was her greatest wish to die on Irish soil. She told me that she felt her deceased family were there to prepare her and help her on her forthcoming journey. She was over ninety and feeling that she was being made aware that her time here on earth was now limited. She began to give away or sell her possessions. Unfortunately, much to our distress, our little rented cottage was totally inadequate to meet the needs of a very elderly lady in the short or long term. My darling mother-in-law passed away two years later at the age of ninety-three while residing in a care home for the elderly back in the United Kingdom.

It is not uncommon, as life comes to a close, to "feel" and "see" deceased loved ones waiting for us prior to our own passing. It would seem to be inherent to all sentient creatures to sense when life as it is known is coming to an end. And as it does so, our deceased friends or family start gathering around us to assist in our passing-over. Spiritual guides and Angels are also there to help us in the crossing over procedure. The presence of deceased loved ones along with Spiritual entities exude love and wisdom at its highest and purest level and are there to calm the dying person relieving any fear we might have. We often hear of people who have survived a near death experience speaking about the presence of a tunnel of light and being reunited with people they know and love. Some people speak of contact with entities from the Spiritual realm. If it is our time to pass over, I have been informed by the Spiritual realm, that after reunion with our loved ones, a life review is followed in accordance with the maturity of our Soul. And the maturity of our Soul depends very much on our actions here in this life and in previous lives through the Law of Cause and Effect and the Law of Consequences that follows. In other words, providing continuation of Soul development until we have attained our higher consciousness, our true Soul enriched by our free-will.

So, do the general masses believe in life after death? Is there still hope or are we too secularised? Surprisingly, according to Andrew Brown of the Guardian, they do. We learn from his blog of {02/07/12} "the decline in religious belief in the UK is matched by increasing faith in life after death, something incompatible with materialism". [8] It would seem therefore, that despite the secular materialistic and irreligious movement of the masses, many people still cling to the belief {or suspicion as Brown would counter} of something to look forward to. Cynically, it could be argued the masses believe in something of the ilk because they hate the thought of being alone or life having no meaning. However, from my own experiences of dealing with the paranormal and the Spiritual realm I can guarantee a type of life after death does indeed exist. I cannot argue categorically though what type of life that could possibly be. But I can tell you that it does exist in another dimension. And while I and thousands like me remain on the fringes of our society for our so-called wacky beliefs, science is slowly catching up. For we learn from the science website Pravda {7/11/2005} "scientists claim life after death exists". [9] This astonishing revelation, {for the science community} comes about after it has been found that hospital patients who had been pronounced dead were able to give description of events and situations surrounding them during their "death" after they had been resurrected back to life. In other words, these patients had been fully aware of what was functioning around them while they were dead. So, it would seem, that many people can, and do experience what it is like to leave their body or to be clinically dead but have been drawn back into their physical bodies to begin life again here on earth. We may thus conclude that their time for passing had not yet come.

So, what is the difference between a ghost and a Spirit? In simple terms, Spirits are those individuals who have gone through the Light and a life review and may come back to observe us or watch over us or share in our experiences here on the earthly plane just as my brother or other members of my deceased family do for me or the deceased family of my mother-in-law did for her. Experiences of Spirit can happen to any one of us because all of us, good or bad have loved ones and Spiritual guides and Angels who care for us and are watching over us continuously. They are with us 24/7. They are attached to us through Love, as Love is the only thing that matters, connecting us all to each other having no ending and no boundary. Love is all Ascending and all-encompassing bringing Peace, Joy, Love and Truth. Spirits are thus here to assist us, warn us or to bring comfort. Spirit only has the best intentions. They make themselves known to work on our behalf. Spirits know we are all individual ones connected with each other through the vehicle of Love and with the other "Greater One". Spirits want to share their experience of the Light assisting in the task of bringing us all into the creation of Light which embodies Peace, Joy, Love and Truth. An enlightened Spirit will come in the presence of Light, exuding Love. And because they come in Peace, Joy, Love and Truth we may know that they are working on behalf of the Angel realm thus making them a Spiritual messenger.

I have been informed by the Spiritual realm that the realm of Hell is a temporary place in accordance with a Soul that is lost. A creation of its own living Hell while residing here on the earthly plane. Many people in their life manufacture their own living Hell through their thoughts, words or actions often generating a living Hell for others to reside in as well, and if they die while living under these negative conditions they will die leaving behind unresolved negative residue. I believe that these lower levels of darkness run parallel to the earthly plane. When we think of all the barbaric atrocities that are perpetrated by human beings against each other, and against other species and planet Earth itself, is it any wonder that many of us experience negative energies while living in this life, because energy is catching, it is contagious! Thus, negative energies produce more negative energies resulting in individuals who become ghosts, individuals who have not undergone the tunnel of Light or a life review. Ghosts belong to Souls whose condition is subjected to a lack of understanding as they struggle with negative residue of their own making. Ghosts still have attachments to this world through such vehicles as emotional trauma, or death via violence or fears or revenge that keep them rooted to the physical world or some other unfinished business. They reside in a self-created prison, a residue of destructive negative energy and no matter what the reason might be, it is up to the Spiritually nourished to assist in the undoing of their dark position. Thus, when we encounter a ghost, many of whom only seek acknowledgement of their existence, we should speak words of comfort to them and send them on their way with peace, blessings, and compassion.

They need to know that turning towards the Light will bring them Peace, Joy, Love and Truth.

One of the best films I have ever watched depicting the difference between a ghost and a Spirit is the film "Ghost". Sam played by Patrick Swayze and Molly played by Demi Moore are two people who are deeply in love. And it is this love all ascending and all transcending and Sam's untimely and violent death that keeps him rooted to the earthly plane in order to save Molly from the dangers she is in. Sam, as a ghost comes across another ghost on the subway played by Vincent Schiavelli who demonstrates how to make things move in the physical world. And later, Sam stumbles upon Oda Mae Brown, played by Whoopie Goldberg an unsuspecting psychic and Spiritual medium who helps him to communicate his words and feelings to Molly. It is only when Sam's job here on earth has been completed, that Molly is safe, and that justice has been seen to be done and all the evil energies that perpetrated his murder have been put to rights, is Sam lovingly and willingly drawn up into the tunnel of Light. His task and his life on earth are over, but his love for Molly lives on as he now journeys fourth as Spirit. So, it is for all of us if we choose.

Chapter 4

Divination or what?

Since Man has walked the Earth, he has been trying to predict his future and understand the world around him. Over time his observations taught him that with specific events or circumstances, certain things would happen within the natural world. For example, animals and insect life would move to higher ground before an earthquake or a huge storm which resulted in massive flooding. The relationship between the tides and the phases of the moon has been known for over 2000 years, and evidence of an understanding of astronomy and time even in the stone-age spans the globe from Stonehenge in England to the ruins of the Mayan civilization. Thus, the weather, the moon, the sun or stars, phenomena of the natural world became predictive tools for how to live and plan one's life. Within these natural phenomena, primitive Man recognised an energy of which he was part. He recognised and utilised his five senses of touch, taste, smell, hearing, and seeing which aided his interpretation of the energies around him, but also recognised and utilised his psychic prowess above all else. Early primitive tribal communities around the world relied on specialists such as medicine men in the Americas, Shamans in Asia and Witch Doctors in Africa and later seers in Greek and Roman cultures for divination practices. Indeed, the English word "auspicious" comes from the Latin "auspex" which means "bird seer" – literally someone who would predict the future based on the observations of the birds. With so many systems and methods for attempting to divine and predict the future, is it possible that something underpins and ties these all together? Are these mere superstitions, or windows into a codex of information that transcends time and space? Are the “Akashic Records” such a concept– a mystical compendium of humanity’s past, present and future experiences that exists in an etheric plane but might perhaps be accessed in some way? Is it possible that mediumship and those that are highly sensitive, psychic souls have the faculty to access such information? From my own experiences I believe it is so.

When I was a child of about 10 years old, a school friend’s mother used to read the tea leaves. In pre-teabag days when a pot of tea was always on the go in most households, it wasn’t unusual to hear of somebody who could “read” the tea leaves. Reading the tea leaves was done predominantly by women, probably because in the main they were housebound, while the men went out to work. Or maybe it was because it was considered too frivolous or irrational for men who had better things to do! These days, thank goodness, these sorts of petty discriminations are rare. Anyone can read the leaves at the bottom of one’s cup or mug after the nectar has been drunk providing you are psychically inclined. My friend’s mum wouldn’t do anything without consulting the tea leaves, especially when it came to major decisions. She would sit at the kitchen table swirling the dregs around the bottom of her teacup while thinking of her question. She would then place a saucer on top of the cup and turn the whole thing upside down, so any trace of liquid would end up in the saucer leaving the tea leaves clinging to the side of the vessel. A picture ensued from the swirling mass of infused tea leaves from whence an answer was always gleamed. This lady seemed to get all sorts of information from her tea leaf pattern from daily concerns to the outcome of more difficult circumstances, a romantic involvement, or of a work or financial nature. The amount of information held within the tea leaves always had me awestruck. Of course, as a child, one could argue I was easily taking in by this so-called

Fairground amusement. But my friend's mother was never short of people seeking out her psychic advice. She was always in great demand among her neighbours and friends because her readings were so accurate. She didn't charge anything, but it was considered lucky to press some silver into her palm after a reading. I remember on one occasion; I had called for my friend on the way to school in the morning. When I got to her house, I found her rushing around in a flustered state shoving books and pencil case into her satchel as I walked into the kitchen.

"What's wrong with you?" I asked.

"We've got a spelling test, remember?" answered my agitated friend.

My friend's mum looked up from her cup of tea and said nonchalantly,

"Oh, don't worry about that darling. "I've consulted the tea leaves and they've told me you'll get through your spelling test with flying colours".

It was a foregone conclusion my friend's mum would be right. My friend Ruth was the top of the class for her spelling test that morning, whereas I failed miserably. It could be argued that this simplistic mundane example was just a coincidence. But Ruth's mother being a serious advocate of the tea leaves would probably have told you, there is no such thing as coincidences. Ruth wasn't normally very good at spelling.

During the early spring of 1967 my parents were thinking of emigrating to Australia for the second time. Uncle Spencer and auntie Doreen were visiting one Sunday along with my cousins, Stephen, Anne, and Jane. Stephen and I were in our late teens whereas our sisters were a few years younger. Having taken Sunday lunch, the adults were still sat around the dining table engrossed in discussions and conversation on the virtues of Australia. We young folk had left the room and gone into the adjoining lounge. Bored and looking for something to do, Stephen suggested we set up a Ouija board. We girls were innocent at the time of what this entailed. But Stephen seemed to know all about it and explained it was a way of contacting the paranormal or supernatural. On his instructions, a pack of cards with the letters of the alphabet on each one was brought out and a wineglass was found. We all knelt on the floor around a small circular coffee table where the cards were laid out around the edge with the wineglass placed in the centre. Because the main topic of conversation was about my parents going to Australia, Stephen suggested we should ask the Ouija board whether they would go or not. Trying to sit perfectly still on the floor, each one of us placed a finger on the stem of the upturned wineglass. Slowly, to our utter amazement, the wineglass started to move around the perimeter of the table. The younger girls started to giggle and accused Stephen and I of pushing the glass, but we swore we weren't, at least I wasn't! But somehow, the glass was moving, first to the letter Y then onto the letter E before finally stopping at the letter S.

"There you go," said Stephen.
"Your parents are going to Australia".

Encouraged by this state of success, we thought we would give the Ouija board another question. I was concerned that my parents were doing the right thing. My own intuition and instinct were telling me it would be a bad choice if they went ahead with their plans. I had already been informed by the Spiritual realm that this would be so. I felt it would be interesting to see whether the Ouija board came up with the same conclusions. So, I asked,

"Will my parents be happy if they go to Australia?"

With fingers still placed on the wineglass, it slowly started to move around the perimeter of the little table again. This time we were all very quiet as the wineglass started to point out the letters N and O. Encouraged still further by this level of success, Stephen wanted to dig a little deeper with his questions.

"Why won't they be happy?" he asked.
"And who are you?"

At this point, this final question seemed to enrage the energy surrounding the Ouija board. The glass started moving erratically beyond our control, around and around the small coffee table gathering speed as it did so until it flew off across the room crashing into the sliding double doors that separated the dining room from the lounge, splintering glass in all directions. The younger girls screamed, and we all leapt up from the floor in a state of shock. The ensuing pandemonium brought the adults shooting out from the adjoining room.

"What the hell is going on? asked my dad.

Sheepishly, I told him, and he went ballistic.

"Don't you ever do that again,' said dad.
"You leave that rubbish well alone".

I found it interesting that my father referred to the Ouija board as rubbish. Yet his verbal tone and body language informed me he had been unnerved by our involvement of inviting the paranormal into his home. If it was rubbish and there was no substance to it, why was he so concerned? As it turned out, my parents did go to Australia and the failure of their plans to capture the Australian dream once again meant their financial position was severely dented. They were back in Britain within two years, poorer but a lot wiser. As for my experience of the Ouija board of which I have never repeated, I have never been sure in my own mind of who was pushing the wineglass around the coffee table that afternoon. Sadly, there has never been an occasion between my cousins and I where we could discuss this matter further. Those of us that attended, what many would regard as a Fairground amusement, have drifted away from each other over the years.

I first saw a reader of the tarot cards in the autumn of 1985. My first marriage was on the rocks, and I was in financial ruin with three little children to support and no one to rely on emotionally or otherwise. The girlfriend to my brother Nigel was in a similar situation the only difference being, her first marriage had already gone through the divorce courts. Having empathy with our experiences and position, we found solace in each other's company. Beverley was to become a good friend for many years to follow. It was Beverley who first introduced me to tarot card readers, a frequent user of such people at that time.

Tarot card readers and other methods of divination have always invited ridicule and suspicion. I have often heard it said that only suckers or those people going through difficult situations and needing support are drawn to using such questionable measures of forecasting the future. The inference being, that one is a loser in life, or a lost soul, or a head-case in line with the tarot card reader - who is more likely than not to be a charlatan profiteering from another person's misery than a genuine mystic. But in my experience, those that ridicule very often haven't been to a tarot card reading or attended any other method of divination, and their ridiculing and suspicion is born out of ignorance, arrogance or perhaps fear! There seems to be a prevailing attitude amongst secular society that if science can't explain it, then it must be a nonsense. The notion that anyone or any form of divination could forecast future events falls into this category.

It may come as a surprise to learn that as a Spiritual medium I should seek to have "my fortune told" by other methods of divination. Surely if I'm in touch with the "other side", information given to me should give me some level of surety, a sort of comfort blanket. But the plain fact is, while I may have my own psychic faculty, I am still very much a human being with my own insecurities and uncertainties - which are not helped by my lack of patience! Psychically, I have always been able to sense the hidden energies around me. Psychically, I have always been able to "see" the visitations visiting me. Psychically, I have always been able to "hear" the voices from the "other side". But it has not always been easy for me to distinguish between what the Spirit world were informing me and my own egotistical desires and lack of confidence. This was certainly the case in the autumn of 1985 following the collapse of my first marriage, which left me an emotional and mental wreck. Feeling utterly insecure at the time with so much uncertainty going on in my life, visiting a tarot card reader (that Beverley insisted was brilliant) might draw upon some reasons to have hope. For don't we all have the need to have hope and reasons to reach out for the future? As it turned out, this tarot card reader was indeed quite brilliant.

Mary Miller, a lady perhaps in her 60s, lived in a little terraced cottage aptly named "Witch House" in a backstreet of a small Dorset town. We might be forgiven for thinking that Sherborne, with its public-school image and middle-class population errs on the side of sensibility, common sense, and practicality- having no time for psychic phenomena and other airy-fairy notions. But we would be mistaken, for Mary Miller was well-known for her accuracy in the area and extremely busy! This lady, whom I had never met before, invited me to sit opposite her in the tiny front living room. There she proceeded to go through the motions of my first tarot card reading, first taking me through the recent past, followed by the current situation, before finally shedding some light on my future which was to include a violent assault on me and my daughter by my abusive mother, a traumatic event which actually came true a few years later which I describe in my unpublished autobiography. The whole reading took just over an hour and was worth every penny of 15 quid even though I was very hard-up at the time. After the card reading, she took my hands in hers and studied them.

"Mm" she said looking intensely at the lines on my right hand.

"I can see the sudden-death cross here".

When pressed for an explanation, Mary Miller went on to tell me, that soon I would lose someone very close to me. This someone would be a male and quite young and had the appearance of a strange colour. She told me his passing would have a tremendous impact on me resulting in a turning point in my life. She said his death is going to impact me "Big Time." She went on to predict not only the despicable behaviour of my mother, but other close relatives as well. She told me to be wary, these people will stab me in the back. She forecast my second marriage to a man who crossed water for his living. She insisted that this man was already known to me, although at the time, there was no such man in my life that I could think of. Nevertheless, she insisted he was there and that he would bring a sense of security, both emotionally and financially. I didn't go out looking, I was too caught up in my daily life bringing up a young family on my own. But by Christmas of that year, I had by chance reconnected with a first cousin, the son of my mother's sister, whom I hadn't seen for years. He was an officer in the Merchant Navy, and by the spring of 1986 we were making plans to marry. I did indeed, already know him. But what I hadn't expected, was that all the people Mary Miller predicted who would come to stab me in the back would come to play a huge role in the demise of my second marriage, including that of my husband himself. This would lay the foundations for a third marriage to take place as "seen" in the cards and me standing alongside another man in the church for the blessing of our wedding. I was utterly gobsmacked at the accurate detail this tarot card reader had given me concerning events and people from my past and in my current situation. It was as if she had been privy to all my darkest secrets or had been a fly on the wall during my life. Having such accuracy to my past and present I had no reason not to believe her forecast for my future. When pressed for a timescale of when future events would begin to unfold, Mary Miller simply said to me,

"How long is a piece of string?"

In the event, much of what she predicted began to reveal itself soon after the reading. Within the year I was married to my cousin, by the end of three years my second marriage was floundering under the strain of backstabbing close relatives and other predicted events. And by the end of seven years, my darling brother had passed away having died of liver failure in which he jaundiced {he went a deep yellow colour} created by his addiction to alcohol. And I was married to my third husband. My brother's death at the age of thirty-one did indeed "impact my life big time". In addition to experiencing a nervous and emotional breakdown, his death opened doors to the Spiritual realm and the endorsement of my Spiritual Mediumship attributes. And yes, my third husband and I did have our wedding blessed in a little village church while we were living in Northumberland. Of course, a cynic might argue, that some of these events took place because they were born out of ideas or notions implanted in my psyche by the tarot card reader such as having our wedding blessed in church. But let's face it, the event may not have taken place particularly for a third marriage unless all other components for the event were in place or available. Unbeknown to me, at the time of the tarot card reading, my third husband and I were to befriend a local vicar who was a very open and liberated soul. In addition, much of what was predicted was beyond my control such as my brother passing away and the actions of other people.

Since 1985 I have met or visited other tarot card readers, psychics, clairvoyants, and Spiritual mediums. In December 1996 while living in Northumberland I visited a Spiritual medium who reduced me to tears as she described my dead brother's physical appearance in accurate detail. She also described my dad's physical appearance and the loving relationship between us including the fact that dad had been in the Royal Air Force. This kindly silver haired lady who was again a stranger sat next to me on a white sofa holding my hand in a bright sunny living room of her modern home. Here, working as a channeller and asking no questions of me beforehand, she passed on accurate information from my deceased brother concerning things that had been imposed on me beyond my will during my lifetime, and things that would encourage me to reach out for the future. This softly spoken petite lady with porcelain skin looked and behaved like an earthbound Angel and without using any fairground paraphernalia to communicate her very accurate information. She just sat there like a concerned friend talking to me. Visiting others with psychic gifts has become my way of gathering reassurance or reinforcing my own psychic and Spiritual messages. These people come from both sexes in all shapes, sizes, and ages, the youngest being Patrick who I met in 2007. Still in his mid-20s he was the first among them to tell me I have inherited the gift of mediumship from two great aunts. He said he could "see" two old dears standing in the wings waiting to assist me when I'm ready. These two great aunts Grace and Mary were sisters to my paternal granny and now do indeed assist me in my Spiritual mediumship development and work.

The one thing all these psychics had in common was that they had been accurate to a fault in the information passed on to me. None of them had wriggled information out of me. In fact, all of them insisted I didn't speak, they didn't even want to know my name or where I had come from. It thus begs the question, from where does the psychic, clairvoyant or Spiritual medium glean his or her information? Are we all mad, psychotic or suffering from delusions? Do we merely have expansive imaginations? How can a tarot card reader "see" our past, present, and future simply by reading a pack of cards garnered with mythological symbols? One might argue that these special, highly gifted people have simply retained their innate sensitivity born of primitive Man, thus enabling them to "read" the energies around them or use psychometry or perhaps even have access to the Akashic records. Is it that predominantly the masses have lost the ability to use instinct and intuition? And what about the notion of free will? Visiting a tarot card reader reminds us of the axiom,

"It's on the cards" undermining the notion that we are truly free!

In other words, if something can be foreseen, then can we assume it was always going to happen.? During the hot weather while I was writing this chapter, I went out into the garden to take a break. Propped up on a sun lounger with my eyes closed I suddenly became aware of my dad's presence. When dad had been alive, he used to love to sit outside on a warm summer's day. Now in his demise, his visit therefore didn't surprise me. We often used to sit in the garden just chatting. Despite the warm sun goose bumps had developed all over my arms as a surge of intense joy hit my solar plexus while at the same time a mental image of his visitation came into my mind.

"Think about the sudden-death cross on your right hand" he said.

My family on the "other side" are very supportive of my writing, dad now being especially encouraging. Very often I find that while I am writing I get an intense feeling that I am being guided and tutored. Questions and answers come into my mind, as the role of teacher and student are brought together. Thinking about what dad had pointed out, a profound Truth suddenly dawned on me. Surely, if I carry the sudden-death cross on my right hand, I can only assume that I was always going to experience at some point in my life, emotional devastation related to the symbol. And this being the case, does it suggest that our lives are predetermined? Once again, we can argue that the tarot card reader, psychic, clairvoyant, and Spiritual medium would not be able to "see" or forecast a future if it wasn't already there to "see". As scary as some people might find it, we can only assume we are all destined to travel down particular roads in life. This puts the notion of free will under scrutiny! However, how far down the road a tarot card reader, psychic, clairvoyant, or Spiritual mediums can "see" is unclear. Some would tell you that their forecast covers the next 12 months, others would put a timescale of several years, but if they are honest, they won't commit themselves. My husband had a reading done 20 years ago and while some of the events predicted have taken place, others are only just coming to fruition. The psychic eye's ability to "see" ahead way into the future is beyond scientific explanation and comprehension. At least for the time being!

There are many things in life which can't be explained or measured by modern science in a laboratory, such as the act of divining for water. Still, nobody can be certain why the bent wire or hazel twig starts twitching over an area of underground water. The act of seeking water for the benefit of survival has evolved with Man right up to the present day. In the summer of 2009, the National Trust in England started courses on dowsing. It created a lot of controversy among the British public many of whom accused the National Trust of wasting public money and resources. [10] This position saddens me because it testifies to the many closed minds that still prevail among the masses. These people have been secularised to the detriment of losing one's innate instincts and intuitions. They have lived in a concrete jungle for far too long, desensitised and detached from their Spiritual selves. No wonder there are so many lost Souls on the earth now. Unless the human population change significantly these damaging attitudes are only likely to get worse. Here I am reminded of the axiom,

"Use it or lose it".

Nevertheless, the courses went ahead gaining popularity among those that attended. Dowsing can be used not only to search for water but also a great number of artefacts and entities, including people. The dowsing rod belonging to my son Daniel went ballistic in the corner of an old house which was reputed to be haunted leaving everyone attending convinced he had tapped into something mysterious! And in holistic healing and medicine, using a crystal pendulum, dowsing is widely used to detect the causes of imbalance which led to poor health. Many people who douse believe this skill rests on instinct and having the ability to tap into the hidden energies around us. In our primeval state, we all had this ability. Sadly, too many people today rely on living in a virtual reality world where instinct and intuition has been suppressed thus now holds no place in the modern world. But thank goodness there are still some people that think otherwise. In 1921 the concept of Ley lines was suggested by an English amateur archaeologist Alfred Watkins although it is thought that the background to this concept is attributed to the English astronomer, Norman Lockyer. Watkin's theory was that these Ley lines were alignments created for ease of overland trekking in line with sight navigation during Neolithic times which had persisted over millennia. In more recent times, unseen by the naked eye, Ley lines have taken on a more Spiritual significance because of their link to hilltops, tumuli, church sites and other traditional places of worship and sanctuary within the British

Isles and other areas around the world. This Spiritual concept is not unlike the Chinese concept of Feng Shui where the placement of certain artefacts, plant life, furnishings within the home or the office or even buildings at a particular angle are an important consideration to invite good chi or energy. Like astrology, dowsing and other acts of divination along with the concept of Feng Shui was laid down by ancient humanity which relied on sight navigation, empirical observation, instinct, and intuition to survive. We might well thus consider Ley lines in the same way. Ancient humanity understood the term,

"Go with the flow".

They understood how to utilise the seasons, working by day, sleeping by night, recognising the importance of observing the moon, the sun, and later other planets as well. Survival relied on instinct and intuition enabling the ability to “read” people, the situation, or the landscape - tapping into the hidden energies around them. Instinct, intuition and empirical experience and observation informed humanity that lesser energies were linked into a Greater Universal energy or Spirit. They were conscious of the subconscious. They were at one with nature and the world around them. In today’s world, for many people this is sadly no longer the case, which is why holistic medication, dowsing, astrology, mediumship, psychics and clairvoyants, tarot cards, palmistry and other forms of divination all invite controversy and ridicule. The age of the teabag has now become a metaphor for humanity who can no longer think or work outside the box. The tea leaves have been caged leaving no room for psychic engaging thus interpretation, understanding and Spiritual fulfilment.

Chapter 5

Astrology

Having studied the subject for the previous three years, I gained a diploma in astrology in 2003. Since then, I have learnt over the years from calculation and analysis of many clients charts that astrology is indeed a divination tool that can be accurate if the correct birth data is used. In its current form, astrology is based on geometry devised by Greek mathematicians and the earlier science of mathematical astronomy of Babylonian civilisation in fifth century BC. Beginning as a pagan science, {there is evidence that the Druids used it}[11] astrology developed down through the ages with religious elements and philosophies, harmonising with Neoplatonic philosophy, Christian, Judaism, Islamic, and Indian theology including occultism of the Renaissance period. As such, today astrology knows no cultural or social divide. It encompasses all religions or belief systems, and sometimes none. It sits comfortably with atheism or humanism, and so in modern Western countries, it remains a popular, if not controversial subject within today's society. Despite its questionable modern scientific credentials, Nicholas Campion in his book "The Dawn of Astrology" estimates around "70% of the adult population reads horoscope columns". And "most people, well over 90%, know what zodiac sign contained the sun at their birth and a significant number probably between 40% and 50% identify with their zodiacal character." {p.9}[12] This quiet hypocrisy then of astrology's readership and following probably explains its longevity. It taps into a perennial human need that refuses to die. Nevertheless, while the sun sign horoscopes might be fun, they can only give a generalisation. They are by no means the full story. To get a true astrological reading for the individual, a correct birth time and birthplace is needed. So, in many ways, I believe the popularisation of sun signs in the media have only added to the scepticism of astrology's critics.

Not too long ago in human history, astrology was considered an excellent tool that helped mankind to determine God's wishes whether it involved physical events or health issues. This prevailing world view, that the heavens reveal meaning to humanity, has continued in the contemporary world in countries such as India. Within Eastern astrology it is argued that our astrological natal charts are maps of karmic imperfections. It is believed these imperfections are brought over from previous lives to be dealt with and rectified in the present life, or if mismanaged, to go on again into further lives. Here we are advised that we can use our natal charts to become better people by casting off our imperfections with each life until we are at one with our God. Astrology was Man's early way of trying to make sense of his life and the environment in which he lived. Observation and calculation became Man's tools which touched the very fabric of their belief systems. Christianity for example, translates Magi in the New Testament concerning the Gospel of Matthew chapter 2 to mean wise-men or more accurately, astrologers who followed the Star of Bethlehem leading them to the infant Jesus. The Star of Bethlehem is traditionally linked to the Star of Prophecy in the Book of Numbers. But the mention of astrologers in the story of the birth of Jesus was problematic in the early church, as astrology was considered demonic. According to S.J Tester, a widely held view, was that the early Christian author Tertullian had argued that astrology was allowed, but only until the time of the gospel, which might explain why in the Gospel according to Luke, there is no mention of Magi or a Star.[13] Yet despite its demonic suspicions, astrology survived within the Christian tradition even through and after the Reformation of the 16th century. Indeed, for the next couple of centuries, astrology flourished. According to James Herschel

Holden, many eminent Christians believed in and practised astrology, thus we could say, promoting it as a specialised subject and giving it academic credentials. People such as Luca Guárico {1476-1558}, a Roman Catholic bishop who was court astrologer to the Popes and to Catherine De Medici {p. 156} and later, William Lilly, {1602-1681} a Protestant preacher who argued astrology was very compatible with Christianity. [14]{p. 174} During the Renaissance period, astrology was considered interwoven with the very fabric of nature making all life on planet Earth and that of the Heavens part and parcel of the same greater universal power. During this era, there was no clear distinction between astronomy and astrology, despite there being a clear distinction between astronomy and physics, the former considered a branch of mathematics within the liberal arts and the latter considered a branch of natural philosophy. Many of astrology's Western proponents during this period drew on the genius and academic qualifications of eminent persons of continental Europe. Persons such as Nicolaus Copernicus {1473-1543}, a Polish mathematician, astronomer, physician, classic scholar, and translator and Tycho Brahe {1546-1601} a Danish nobleman, astronomer, and alchemist. While Johannes Kepler {1571-1630} assistant to Tycho Brahe, a German mathematician and astronomer whose works provided one of the foundations for Isaac Newton's theory of universal gravitation. Johannes Kepler described his new astronomy as celestial physics, an excursion into Aristotle's metaphysics and a supplement to Aristotle's work, "On the Heavens". These works transformed the ancient tradition of physical cosmology by treating astronomy as part of a universal mathematical physics. Thus, it could be said, these eminent personages were key figures in early scientific revolution. Sadly, within science, as the different disciplines evolved and developed, astrology was downgraded.

In the modern world it is often assumed that anyone who believes in or follows astrology is on the fringe of mainstream society. It presupposes we are against science and technology, when in fact the opposite is true. Our hearts and minds are open, just as scientists are supposed to be, to all possibilities and potentials. When one studies astrology and works with it for many years, one comes to realise there is something in it. It grabs you, and you want to find out more. Ignorantly, many people believe astrology is rubbish simply because they are led to believe so by scientists such as Professor Brian Cox. Yet astrologers are not far removed from scientists in that there is the urge to find out more, to investigate, research, and seek to find answers. You cannot claim something is rubbish until you have worked with it and/or researched it. Surely, that is what the discipline of science is supposed to do? Science is developing all the time, as is its instruments, it is on a learning curve. After all, it wasn't so long ago, with the development of the telescope, that Galileo Galilei {1564-1642} could build on the hypotheses of Nicolaus Copernicus {1473-1543} and earlier astronomers such as Aristarchus of the third century BC, that the Earth and planets revolve around the Sun at the centre of our solar system. Until that time, most subscribed to the notion that the Sun and planets revolved round the Earth. Thus, as a young discipline, science still has much to learn! The notion then that we could be influenced in any way by the energies of the planets seems ludicrous to any level-headed, rational thinking human being, right? And yet science now informs us that the cosmos is full of energy. Everything in the cosmos radiates energy. Everything on planet Earth radiates energy. We are all energy. Energy is contagious. Energy incites energy in positive and/or negative ways. Thoughts are energy, which is why thoughts can travel. The energies of our existence are all around us. We can all learn to read this energy when we know how. I am not a scientist, nor do I pretend to understand the disciplines of cosmology, astronomy, physics, or mathematics, but as a psychic and

Spiritual medium/healer my instincts inform me, we are all influenced by the energies above and around us. Some of the energies have a subtle influence on us, while others have a more drastic influence like the energies of thought processes that can incite violence or hatred in crowded situations. Other thought processes can be positive, we all know of people we like the company of, and others we prefer to ignore! All living things are influenced or affected by the energies of the Earth's weather systems whether good or bad. Suffering from Seasonal Affective Disorder, I know from experience how my moods can change according to the weather. During the winter months when many days are dark and gloomy, I find it hard to keep my spirits lifted. But when the sun shines and the daylight hours are long, my mood is bright and cheery. Many people will complain of feeling thick-headed or even suffering headaches or migraines as a precursor to a thunderstorm. Indeed, it was known during the days of British occupation in India that the British troops used to "go doolally" during the oppressive weather conditions before the monsoons broke. Deolali was the site of a troop station and sanatorium in India where the troops were sometimes stationed for months before coming home, and to "go doolally" become a popular colloquialism in British culture to indicate someone who has become mentally disturbed or is not thinking straight.

The notion then, that the energies of planets, the Sun and the Moon could have any effect upon us draws hot debate from both sides, thus inviting ridicule or quiet open-mindedness or belief. There seems to be two camps of thought. Thus, currently the jury is still out that the Moon has an influence over sentient behaviour. Despite this theory being disputable, not so long ago in 1973, in his book "Supernature" Lyall Watson draws on historical research to show that Homo sapiens are components to nature because they are affected like everything else in nature by the different phases of the Moon. He found not only was the

Moon the basic rhythm of life, the lunar cycle thought to be responsible not only for the movement of the tides, but in correlation to that, the flow of the menstrual cycle, the flow of blood in general, the times of birth, and how the effects of the full Moon on human behaviour records that crimes with strong psychotic motivation does indeed rise. Leonard Ravitz, a neurologist, and psychiatric consultant discovered a direct physiological connection between Man and the Moon which could explain these correlations. He suggested that the Moon modifies the Earth's magnetic field that brings about changes precipitating crisis in people whose mental balance is already precarious. He says, "whatever else we may be, we are all electric machines". "Thus, energy reserves may be mobilised by periodic universal factors {such as the forces behind the Moon} [15] Once we take on board the notion that the human species is an animal despite its perceived superiority born out of ignorance and arrogance and that it is no different to all other sentient creatures on planet Earth, in that all life is made-up of atoms and all life is electric energy. And so, as an electric component it becomes easier to understand how recent research has found that different colours radiate different frequencies of energy that stimulate different rates of growth in plants, thus taking our food production down a futuristic route. [16] The theory that even plant life has a correlation with the energies of the planet was picked up by the 17th century herbalist and apothecary Nicholas Culpeper who combined herbal medicine and astrology by ascribing a ruling planet to each plant. [17] In more recent times, organic farmers in the UK and Ireland have taken up the gauntlet by applying the principles of biodynamic farming. A form of farming in which livestock are treated with homeopathic remedies while astronomical calendars and signs of the zodiac play a key role in determining the appropriate time for sowing and harvesting. Again, we see a link between all life on planet Earth and astrology. I believe we cannot disassociate ourselves from the energies of the natural world, because we are part of it.

And because we know many creatures of the natural world are stimulated and/or affected to behave in a certain way on the night of a full Moon, such as the hatching of baby turtles or the spawning of a coral reef, why should we think we are any different? The frequency of energy is all around us, above us and within us.

In his book, "Astrology" second edition 1979, Jeff Mayo, {now deceased} founder to the Mayo School of Astrology, wrote of the findings to 15 years of research into this subject. During this period, Jeff Mayo along with the collaboration of Professor Hans Eysenck, Director of the Department of psychology in the Institute of Psychiatry in London, researched the astrological tradition that certain zodiac signs were extrovert and certain zodiac signs were introvert. Questionnaires were sent out to thousands of people, the data accumulated by a pilot study at first overseen by Mayo and analysed manually, then later by a second study overseen by the professor analysed through a computer. Both methods came up with the same results, that there is a relationship between personality and birth date. Clearly Professor Eysenck was gobsmacked at these findings. "I must admit that this was a great surprise to me". "My instinctive scepticism and dislike of anything mystical had led me to expect unrelieved failure from any investigations of astrological predictions". "To find some solid fact in the astrological field was surprising and not entirely welcome!" Other areas of research by radio meteorologists found 93% accuracy, that electromagnetic storms correlated to traditional angular relationships of the planets and the Sun. And that the correlation of sunspot cycles with phases of maximum or minimum sunspot activity with rainfall and certain epidemics left scientists and meteorologists more than intrigued! In the same way, a study of tree growth recorded by their annual growth rings was shown to correspond with the fluctuations of rainfall cycles corresponding to the 11-year rhythm of sunspots. [18] In the "Science" Journal of 1962 {vol. 137} two groups of scientists from America and Australia researched thousands of records from 1500 weather stations over the period of 1900 to 1949 into the influence of the Moon's phases upon rainfall. Neither group knew each other, nor of their research, yet they came up with the same results, that heavy rain occurred most frequently in the weeks immediately following a New Moon and Full Moon. Jeff Mayo informs us that "The result so surprised the Australian group that they refrained from publishing observations for fear of ridicule from other scientists!" And in the scientific journal "Nature" {Supplement No. 4, Vol 184} the retired geophysicist of Munich University, Dr Rudolf Tomaschek reported findings of a study into 134 most powerful earthquakes during the period of 1904 to 1906. During this time, the planet of Uranus, astrologically associated with disruptive, unexpected, and explosive occurrences was within 15° of the upper or lower Meridian of an earthquake's epicentre far more frequently than chance would allow. As Jeff Mayo argued, "With scientific evidence that the cyclic motions and interrelationships of the Sun, Moon and planets correspond to growth patterns in vegetative forms of Earth life and with meteorological phenomena, one cannot discount the possibility of the human being, physically and psychologically also being a part of these interrelated patterns of Earth and cosmic energy systems." [18] The theory that we could be psychologically influenced by the planets at the time of our birth was also researched by the French psychologist and statistician, Michael Gauquelin. With the help of his wife and many others they undertook the enormous task of analysing the astrological birth data of thousands of people. It was found that in careers and vocation, the placement of the planet of Mars in natal charts highlighted sport champions, while the placement of Saturn, highlighted famous doctors and scientists, while the placement of Jupiter, highlighted famous actors. They also analysed the birth data of 30,000 French parents and their children which highlighted that a planetary hereditary effect does exist. [18] The notion that we can be psychologically assessed by analysing birth data astrologically may indeed unnerve the sceptics of astrology. But a trained astrologer understanding and analysing an astrological birth chart knows full well how this information can highlight the complexities and contradictions of the human persona. Indeed, a modern professionally trained astrologer would find empathy with the remarks of Dr Carl Jung. In 1948 he wrote to the editor of the Indian astrological magazine, confessing his faith in astrology. He wrote, "I've been interested in this particular activity of the human mind since more than 30 years" "I must say that I very often found that the astrological data elucidated certain points which I otherwise would have been unable to understand". [18]

Some astrologers would argue thus that astrology should be treated as a science. But currently, astrology is not an exact science, and so should not be judged as one. Like its scientific cousins before it, astrology now stands alone, and so it should until science can catch up. For me at least, astrology is a science of nature, both sublime and subliminal that goes beyond current scientific explanation - it is an instinct of a creative force far greater than us. There are many creative forces that can be found in various forms of the natural world, such as the awe-inspiring scene of a sunrise or sunset, a rainbow, or a starlit canvas under a night sky. These beautiful wonders of the natural world can only take place under the right conditions, the same as Love, another creative energy. The word "inspire" means to take in our breath. The word "expire" is to let our breath out. When I am out walking on my own in the countryside or along an empty beach, I very often get inspiration with creative thought as I take in clean unpolluted air. Air that is devoid of negative energy tainted by manufactured toxins or the company of other humans. That is why, when we exercise, we cleanse not only our bodies through movement, but we cleanse our minds, we are energised, we cleanse our Souls, and we become inspired. We take our breath in; we then naturally breathe it out. The word inspire is from the Latin "inspirare" literally meaning "to breath into" and was originally used in the sense of a Divine Being imparting or "breathing in" an idea or truth to someone.

To become inspired also suggests it catches our breathe, which we might find in human craftsmanship as well. Such as the execution of a beautiful painting, an architectural design, the pattern on a piece of china, a piece of beautiful jewellery, a dance routine, the composition of a piece of music or poetry. We become inspired through instinct; it is a personal sublime force. We cannot scientifically measure or prove that these creative forces and energies exist. Any more than we can prove or measure or contain and box-up the energies of love or hate. They lay unseen, untouched until they are expressed in the physical, material world. Thus, for me, the use of mathematical calculations to determine the placement of the planets at the time of one's birth is a creative art born of instinct. An art that enables me to decipher the energies around us, above us and within us. Astrology is no longer considered a predictive tool, but a vehicle which enables the modern astrologer to decipher a client's potential psychological urges i.e., the energies that take us down potential roads. An astrological reading of the individual's character can highlight their potential positive and/or negative urges. And we are stimulated or encouraged to activate these potential urges in accordance with the energies of the said planets marking out the heavens at the time of our birth. Can this be possible you might ask yourself? Science cannot prove it, and neither can the astrologer in scientific terms. But as an astrologer who has worked on many client's charts, I have found my readings and interpretations to be correct more often, than not, the latter because the client had given me the wrong birth data.

Thus, an astrological reading can highlight potential leanings towards a certain type of career, relationship, hobby, health problem and/or creative or spiritual aspirations. This is not to take a fatalistic stance, because the belief among many modern-day astrologers is that our potentials give us a choice, indicating free will. The subject of fate and free will has baffled and divided many theologians, philosophers, scientists, and astrologers down through the centuries. Perhaps we should consider James Herschel Holden's theory, that fate and free will are two sides to the same coin, {p.270} [14] which I tend to agree with. This could be considered as cancelling out true free will, because we are all restricted in accordance with our potential urges. In other words, we are astrologically programmed and true free will is but a human fallacy. The evidence of this is clear to me, when we look around the world and see how different we all are and the different roads we all take, and the different worldviews thereof.

Even the most hardened sceptic will know his birth sign. Since the end of the Second World War, through magazines and newspapers, daily horoscopes of our sun signs have been a favourite pastime for many. Astrology seems to undermine our rationality by tapping into an idle curiosity even for those that claim not to believe in it. It helps fulfil the hope that better things lie on the horizon or perhaps it aligns with a sense of self-identity. Astrology is a cosmic clock that teaches us, there is a time and place for everything. It is an instinct, an intuitive creative force, a coded language of universal energies of cosmic law and order. The universe is governed by cosmic law and order. Planet Earth and all life thereof is governed by it and will self regulate accordingly which is what climate crisis is all about. When Pluto entered Capricorn in November 2008 correlating in that year with the banking crisis, astrologers were not surprised and knew we were in for some tough times over the next 13 years as Pluto brings power and wealth, but also represents disruptions, disease and destroys the old order to make room for the new when life as we know it becomes unsustainable. Pluto is linked to the laws of change and transformation through death, death of a situation, event or physically thus rebirth. One always follows the other. And so, Pluto is the portal to Spirituality, the "Other World." He represents our psychic intuitive tendencies. Capricorn represents the material world within relationship to gardening, farming, the natural world, wildlife, and other species, and our relationship with all these matters, thus the natural environment and the climate itself. Pluto in Capricorn will show how humanity has exploited Mother Earth and all her children for financial gain. Until January 2024 when Pluto moves into Aquarius, humanity will be forced to address its responsibility towards all matters under Capricorn and any diseases that may be rampant will persist and bring death in its wake. On 21st December 2020 we will experience the great conjunction between Jupiter and Saturn, Saturn linked to the Law of Cause and Effect while Jupiter is linked to the Law of opportunity teaching humanity how they must learn from their past experiences and now plan for a better future. While Jupiter longs for expansion and better times, Saturn will implement restrictions and limitations bringing together a sense of Brotherhood in humanity which might rise to the challenges through scientific discovery. When Pluto goes into Aquarius, the sign of Brotherhood, we may well find the answers to some of the world's problems scientifically and technically, while at the same time evolving our mindset to greater awareness of our connection to nature and all other life on planet Earth, helping humanity to re-evaluate their priorities. Thus, Brotherhood will come to mean, not just Brotherhood of humanity, but inclusive of all Life, a Spiritual awareness that all Life is linked.

So, for me, astrology should not be equated with science, because I think of it as a subliminal creative force that we can read if we learn how. It is about tapping into the energies around us and learning to read the forces of nature in our daily existence, just as our forbearers did to survive. It allows us to know intuitively, that when we look up into the sky, that we come from "somewhere out there", the draw, the instinct that urges space travel. Tragically though, these days, everything must be "proved" by science, and if it can't be "proved", it is regarded as worthless. Like an old traditional farmer who can read the signs of nature and the weather to arm himself with information on how best to perform the next task in relation to sowing or harvesting crops or moving his animals to higher or lower ground. Computer technology can now forecast the weather, days sometimes weeks in advance. Yet they still get it wrong sometimes. As do the predictions of so-called experts such as economists, political analysis, even our physicians! For those that rely on the weather for their work, their subliminal knowledge can still work best at a local level. It is about tapping into the energies around us and learning to read the coded language of nature. In much the same way, Astrology relies on a mathematical coded language built-up and developed over thousands of years, passed down over many generations, cultures, societies and countries of subliminal knowledge. I think of astrology as a mathematical "Art" in line with Pythagoras's insight {c580-500 BC} into the relationship between numbers and the universe. Interestingly, Pythagoras also saw a Spiritual link here in line with my own philosophy. I think astrology is hugely Spiritual because I believe it informs us of our challenges between our Ego and our Spirit thus encouraging us to progress Spiritually, resting its case on the hidden energies above and around us and within us just as reflexology, acupuncture and acupressure rest their case on the hidden energy channels within us. {Chakras} Science still cannot explain these holistic therapies, but those of us that have availed of them know they work. These energies are all around us and within us and are part and parcel of a greater universal energy, the Ultimate Reality or God, a colloquialism known by many different names, the very essence of all things created. As a psychic and Spiritual medium/healer also in touch with the hidden energies within and around us, it is my firm belief that astrology can help us to become better people through understanding ourselves and others in a light that encourages harmony in human relationships and other life forms, thus benefits the world at large. With such an influx of multitude information and calculation, astrology has stood the test of time because it has been developed and built on the work and observation of those gone by over two millennia ensuring its continued longevity while science is still learning and seeking answers and attempting to catch up! We should be careful we do not become too secular and scientific at the expense of who we really are! Sadly, as scientific critics continue to spout rubbish on a subject, they know nothing about, society will continue to grovel in the dark treating astrology "For entertainment purposes only".

Chapter 6

Mindfulness

To be mindful is an emotional non-reactive state helping us to focus on attention of purpose. As a lifelong Spiritual medium, I know the power of meditation and mindfulness as it is the key that unlocks all else that flows from Spirit. It is who I am, I do not have to try. Being a creature of solitude, meditation and being mindful of the moment and its energies thereof comes naturally to me - I have one foot in this world, and one foot in the other! As a child, my communications with Spirit and other hidden energies made it appear I was lost in a world of my own, and consequently, I was always being called a dreamer by my mother and my schools. But this label only shows adult ignorance and arrogance born of social and cultural indoctrination. As children, we are all in touch with the hidden energies around us, and it is only over time that we are conditioned to believe they are a nonsense. Consequently, mindfulness and meditation and thus the ability to read energies around us is largely lost to the general population. Now instead of feeling lonely and different from the world at large, I find I am on a Path to teach others how to find themselves again. How to read the energies of everything around us in our daily life, whether in this world, or those that might be visiting from the "Other World".

Many people assume there is a world of difference between those that claim to be psychic and/or Spiritual and those that claim they are not - yet this is far from true. For most of us, apart from the rare exception, are psychic or Spiritual to a greater or lesser extent at the time of our birth. It is just that modern life, in its current form, has us rushing about, focusing on things that are detrimental to our Spiritual selves. We live within a manufactured world made of concrete - isolating us from sensory information. Millions of people around the globe, especially in the Western world, now exist on a conveyor belt, convinced by social and cultural indoctrination that a great education will guarantee a great career, which will guarantee financial security, which will guarantee all the trappings that wealth can bring, which will guarantee happiness. We rise in the mornings woken by the alarm, grab the smart phone, check our emails, send a few texts, perhaps flash up the laptop or the television. Shower or have a bath, get dressed, grab a coffee or a cup of tea and a quick bite to eat, if we are lucky! There is not time for anything more - there is a bus or train to catch, as we join the throngs of other robots, or perhaps the car provides independence, only to get stuck in gridlock again. And like an alien appendage to the physical human body, all the while we stay in touch with the wider world and with each other through our electronic devices, believing we cannot survive without them. We eat, drink, and communicate on the hoof, there is no time for grace and social etiquette. Gone are the days for a lot of people when they sit at a table for their evening meal as a family, discussing their day's activities. Now they are more likely to come home to an empty house at different times of the day, only to sit perched on the edge of the sofa with their electronic device or watching TV having grabbed something quick from the microwave. We live in a world of limitless constant distractions, attempting to do half a dozen things at once. Cook the dinner, surf the web, watch the children, throw the laundry in the washing machine, then toss it in the tumble dryer and all the while, catch up on our favourite Netflix show. Some selfish maniacs even try using their mobile phone while driving their vehicle, putting not only their own life at risk, but more importantly, innocent lives of others. Hand free car phones have also been shown to be a distraction while driving. Time is a premium, a rare commodity in the modern world, rushing us here, there, and everywhere, only to find in the end, we are all in the same queue!

A run in the park or in the countryside or along the beach no longer provides a sense of well-being. Too many people are closeted off from natural sensations by headphones providing man-made noise via their alien friend. We seem now unable to communicate unless through our devices, devoid of all other sensory information. The Internet and its social platforms while having their advantages, often only project perfection: from artfully angled holiday selfies, filtering out negativity, the carefully edited description of our fun times or persona exerting huge energies to live up to the world of commercial advertising (or simply the false lives presented by our online peers). We live in a virtual world instilling unrealistic high expectations. For many people, there is no way of knowing what is real or what is true, so for many people they believe everyone is happy and leads a perfect life - except them! Cut off from sensory information, the human-race become easy targets for fake news. Like a chattering monkey, our minds are constantly busy, looking back, looking forward, worried about things that have been and gone, or might never happen, consumed with incidental trivia, chatting on about this and that, but never mindful of the present. The chaos of our modern world gives us a false perspective against things that really matter. Yet when we take a moment to stand back, to take a breath and look around us, to be mindful of the moment, we find another worldview.

Children live in the moment; they are mindful of what they are doing and feeling and express themselves accordingly. In that moment, they are not worried about the past or the future, but only in the now situation. Even a child from an unhappy background can become absorbed in their play, finding respite from things that upset them. My own childhood, although happy in many ways was tainted by my cruel vindictive mother who often targeted me and others that I loved with her malicious behaviour. Yet despite this I found much pleasure and solace in the welfare of animals and the countryside. Being a child tutored by Spirit, I was always mindful of the sights, sounds, smells, and energies surrounding me, losing myself in those precious moments. Many people who have become successful in their adult life came from an unhappy childhood but used their ability to be mindful and focused on their creativity to escape.

I believe the best tool to achieve mindfulness is through the art of meditation. Through meditation, we become mindful, we are existing in the moment. We become aware of our sensations, which provide us information of the potentials within us and the environment around us and being mindful helps us to read these energies. By focusing on a touch, texture, sound, smell, image or taste, the mind is prevented from wandering. By preventing the mind from wandering, together with stripping away the emotional component of any given situation, we feel less stressed, less emotionally bogged down or anxious about any potential misgivings connected to the past and/or of the future. This then provides a circular platform which means we are more capable of living in the moment and enjoying life for what it is, rather than worrying about the past or what might go wrong at some later date. Taking this approach means we are more likely to see, hear, or understand things that we might otherwise have missed. In this way, mindfulness becomes a useful tool to be used effectively in our modern busy lives when we need to listen to others or assimilate lots of complicated information. Thanks to recent research in neuroscience, meditation and mindfulness is no longer seen as the preserve of Tibetan monks or hippies of a bygone age, but rather as a useful tool to release inner tensions, bringing harmony and balance between the emotions, the mind, and the body. Meditation and mindfulness are therefore now seen as a tool to address many emotional, mental, or psychological health concerns born of stress, that we know can lead to more serious diseases. The issue of stress is a big factor in our modern world which can cloud our judgements and deplete our energies, and is now being taken more seriously, not only by the medical profession, but in our places of work and education.

We now read in the press, that some healthcare practitioners are concerned that stress is responsible for the current rate of sperm decline and that if trends continue the human-race will be infertile in 50 years. With psychologists and psychiatrists having concerns that the human population, especially the young, has become addicted to electronic devices (more to the point their smart phones) creating huge levels of stress as a result, we might indeed heed this warning. Perhaps ironically, while many people are concerned about an overpopulated planet, things might change very quickly if stress is not addressed. Thankfully, changes are occurring in some quarters. Schools are now teaching pupils as young as primary school-age the art of meditation and mindfulness, as are global international companies such as Google. So, how do we benefit from meditation and mindfulness? To understand how, we need to understand the physiology of our brain and how it and our mind functions.

Our brains have two hemispheres, left and right. It is suggested by some that left brained people tend to be more logical, practical, objective, analytical, most often good at maths and science. While right brained people tend to be more intuitive, psychic, Spiritual, creative, artistic, and philosophical. However, this view is largely unsubstantiated by scientists, although some functions such as speech and spatial processing do indeed appear to exhibit laterality (the function is located within one hemisphere more than the other). The prime facilitator of information between our two brain hemispheres, about 10 cm beneath the cortex, is the Grand Central station, a bundle of nerves called the corpus callosum. Within these two hemispheres lies the hippocampus, one for each side of the brain, a tiny organ the shape of a little seahorse, for which it is named. It appears insignificant for its size, yet scientists now know that the hippocampus is the brain's most important region for storing and retrieving memories. Furthermore, this region is neuroplastic, meaning it can strengthen and grow new cells no matter what our age. In addition, scientists have found that one way to encourage the strength and growth of new cells of our hippocampus is through meditation. No longer are we required to accept "brain fog," short-term memory loss and diminished memories and mental function as we grow older, for scientific studies of meditators have shown that their brains are always well formed with highly developed hippocampus's. Using the latest in MRI brain scanning, Harvard university researchers found that meditation in both the short and long-term increased the neural mass our grey matter of the brain, which is associated with long and short-term memory, while simultaneously quietening the electrical impulses associated with anxiety, depression, fear and anger. When the latter happens, our bodies get flooded with the stress hormone cortisol, which long-term can be detrimental to our physical, mental, and emotional well-being. Long-term stress can create or worsen long-term health problems, such as arthritis or rheumatism, heart disease, Alzheimer's disease, dementia and is strongly associated with premature death. However, scientific research found that meditation not only reduced the flow of cortisol, and thus reduces stress related health conditions, but also brought balance between our two hemispheres, and because the negative impulses no longer took precedence, the feel-good factor of the prefrontal cortex was stimulated.[19] No longer are we required to accept the brain that we were born with or now have.

Through meditation, science has shown we can grow new brain cells, reshaping our grey matter, laying a new foundation of neural pathways, accessing the whole brain, boosting our brainpower, our IQ, our creativity, our intuition and psychic attributes, our Spirituality, our memory, and intelligence.

Not only is our brain separated into two hemispheres of left and right, but it is also made up of other distinct areas. The hindbrain is responsible for our basic functions of living and breathing, the midbrain being more advanced and involved in emotional responses, and the forebrain yet more complicated and where our psychological urges, working memory and language centres are situated. Similarly, our Mind also has different levels of consciousness and is in my opinion a separate entity from the brain. The mind is an intangible phenomenon that links all Life together into a Oneness from which we started. Call it what you will - The Universal Force, a Spiritual Force, the Ultimate Reality. The brain is merely a tool used by the mind, which exists as an energy that cannot be contained, but it is able to access different levels of our self and the Self from which we come.

The first level is our Conscious Mind, associated with Beta brainwaves. Here the Ego exists, powered by the willpower and the educated mind. It contains superficial ideas, likes, and dislikes, analytical and logical thought and planning but also critical negative self-talk, indoctrinated beliefs, and short-term memory. As a result, here also lies the key to controlling our self-esteem, judgements, and selfish and inconsiderate thoughts, and indeed our stress – for in fact stress is not the result of external pressures, more how our mind reacts to such external pressures. Here, through meditation by accessing our Alpha and Theta brainwaves, we can access our Subconscious Mind which lies just below. In the Subconscious Mind our insight exists, our intuition, and our psychic telepathic ability. Those gut feelings, our true desires, when properly accessed and understood can unlock our self-healing ability and true inner peace, and in many cases may the true genius within waiting to be dug out to reveal our life solutions. Here, accessed via meditation, we can change our thought patterns, becoming more creative and inventive, and access our imagination and visualisation. Here, lies our dream state, coded messages from our Higher Self and the Spirit World. Thus, through meditation, we become more compassionate, kinder, tolerant, and Spiritual in the truest sense. Lastly, at the third level, we find our deeper Subconscious Mind powered by Delta brainwaves, the slowest. By learning meditation, we can access and utilise these Delta brainwaves to access our Highest Self. The core of who we really are, our primal instincts, the ability to make a true Spiritual connection that gives access to collective consciousness. There is no separateness. Here we are at one with each other, the Universe, and the Ultimate Reality. Here devoid of mental, physical, or material concerns, these concepts have no meaning. Here, meditation can strengthen the immune system thus help the body in regeneration. And so, meditation not only helps us to access who we really are, it helps us to be mindful in who we can become.

One way we can retrieve what might be lost, to prepare the body for meditation, is through the practise of yoga. Over the last 30 years, following a warm bath, I have practised Hatha yoga in the evenings in preparation for meditation. The word yoga is derived from the Sanskrit root Yui meaning, "Harnessing horses to the chariot". Simply put, this terminology means, liberating oneself from the clutches of our five physical senses, enabling us to be at one with the Divine Reality. Hatha yoga is perhaps the most popular form of yoga in the Western world which involves postures and exercises that help to revive dormant energies. And as we learn and develop the postures and exercises of Hatha yoga, we are more able to release negative energies and address them, leaving room to awaken positive energies that have been submerged, or for new positive energies to develop. Hatha yoga is an excellent tool to clear and unclog our inner energy channels, our meridians. With regular practice, yoga is an excellent precursor to meditation, helping to obtain a healthy body, a happy state of mind, and a sharp intellect.

But for many people in the modern world, taking themselves off the conveyor belt in the first instance might not be easy. Some would argue, they do not have time to start a program of yoga or meditation to become mindful. Yet meditation and mindfulness does not have to be something you put special time aside for. Meditation and mindfulness can be habit forming and fit very easily into modern daily life. It doesn't mean we have to set time aside to sit cross legged repeating a mantra with our eyes closed, or fingering beads to concentrate our focus, and it doesn't have to mean we use our holiday time to book into a Spiritual retreat. It does not mean we need to embrace Buddhism or Hinduism, for meditation and mindfulness has been practised across all religious spectrums and sometimes none. But we can learn, as a Buddhist monk does, to become aware, to become mindful of the moment in our day-to-day activities as a form of mind training. In our daily activities, we can become mindful of the moment, on the bus, on the train, stuck in gridlock on the road, on awakening for the day. Instead of reaching for the electronic device, breath in through the nose to the count of ten, hold it to the count of ten, release through the mouth to the count of ten, relax. Allow yourself to be calm, be conscious of your breath, be mindful of the moment. Repeat several times when you can. Relax. If you cannot get to the count of ten, begin with the count of five. This simple meditative exercise can be fitted anywhere at any time into your daily life. For meditation can also be called contemplation, an internal effort to self-regulate the mind. And where it is possible, take a moment to be quiet, allow the peace of the moment to absorb you. Do not be afraid of silence, for silence really is not silent, it is full of energy, full of vibrations that over time, you can learn to read. So, the next time a loved one who was passed over suddenly comes to mind, along with a picture of them in your mind's eye, and you get a sensation that they've just walked in the room, they probably have! This will be the result of developed meditation and mindfulness that has sharpened your perception and sensory information enabling you to access other dimensions.

Through meditation and mindfulness, loneliness is non-existent. There is no death, only energy which is infinite. When we learn to be mindful, we expose ourselves to the richness of the moment, the richness of all energies thereof. The colours of the rainbow, the beauty of butterfly wings, the raindrops on the window, the snowflakes falling, the scent of a flower, the warmth of the sun on our face, the song of a bird, the sight of a bumblebee collecting pollen. In Hatha yoga, we become liberated from our five senses enabling a pure state of meditation to take place. Thus, yoga cleanses us from inside out. Then, in our cleansed state, our senses are renewed and awakened again. Our sight, taste, hearing, touch, and smell are enhanced as is our sixth sense, our intuition, our psychic/telepathic attributes, our Spirituality. But even without yoga, we can practise mindfulness. We may find it difficult being mindful in our place of work, but we can become mindful in other ways during our daily activities. Through a creative hobby for example, such as working on a piece of jewellery or a piece of wood, pottery, or metal, observing the grain, the colour, feeling the texture, losing our self in the moment. The same can be achieved while we are cooking, baking, painting on canvas, playing a musical instrument, sewing, or gardening or simply walking or sitting and observing nature. Any activity or creative hobby that entails focus and mindfulness. Just sitting on a park bench watching the ducks or the squirrels is a mindful exercise. Lose yourself in the moment, be mindful of this enchanted world. And as we lose ourselves in the moment, emotionally detached through mindfulness, we awaken all sensory information enabling us to become better guardians of each other, the environment, the climate, our planet Earth, and all life thereof. Thus, we become more compassionate, more tolerant, more considerate, kinder, and loving, more able to understand each other and the needs of all life on planet Earth. Here lies the root to Real happiness. To connect to the moment, to absorb the moment in its most simplistic, organic form. To be mindful through meditation exposes another worldview.

Chapter 7

The Healer

When we are ill, our first port of call is to visit our doctor or other medical provider. Among the pleasantries when we enter their surgery, we are asked, "what can I do for you?" We sit there explaining how we are feeling and what symptoms we might have. They listen to our concerns, perhaps taking our blood pressure, perhaps examining the area of our body that is giving us problems. Usually, unless we specifically say, an orthodox general practitioner will not ask us, "How are you feeling inwardly today?" "How is your Spirit?" "Are you happy with your life, are there areas in your life giving you concern or worry?" "Do you feel content and secure?" "Are you feeling depressed?" With growing human population, so the demands on the social and health systems get stronger, and perhaps it comes as no surprise that our healthcare providers (especially physicians) are now known to be overstretched, and with a tremendous workload that leaves many of them unable to ask after their patient's mental, emotional, or psychological well-being.

As a result of being unable (or unwilling) to ask about and address underlying Spiritual, emotional, or psychological needs, it seems that all too often the patient leaves with a prescription to manage symptoms, without consideration of other underlying factors. In some cases, they may be contributing to the symptoms – but in others they may be directly causal! We know that people are unique in their DNA make-up and their psychological expressions, even though we all look similar outwardly. Although our bodily functions may be the same, we are in fact unique from each other, individualized physically and by mind, heart and Spirit. The resulting widespread use of pharmacological interventions is well-known to result in people suffering from side effects, drug allergies, and even fatal reactions – and these are even more tragic if the medications are unnecessary. But where is the evidence that our emotional state can impact our physical health?

Many of us can relate to the concept of a "tension headache", where a very real and tangible symptom is borne out of nothing other than the power of our mind. The feeling of "butterflies in the stomach" before an exciting event, or the crushing ache of a "broken heart" that can be so severe that it leads to physical changes in the heart shape and function (known as Takotsubo cardiomyopathy). Elevated levels of chronic stress can contribute to high blood pressure, resulting in physical injury to the heart, blood vessels, brain, lungs, liver, kidneys – even our eyesight can suffer! People infected with the human immunodeficiency virus progress faster to AIDS if they are depressed, and cancer survival has also been linked to mental attitude. To bring this all together, one recent study looking at 35 years of follow-up for over 13,000 people in retirement found that a "positive mental attitude" was associated with a 20-25% reduction in the risk of death! (Annlia Paganini-Hill, Claudia H. Kawas, and María M. Corrada. Positive Mental Attitude Associated with Lower 35-Year Mortality: The Leisure World Cohort Study. J Aging Res. 2018; 2018: 2126368)

And so, we know our thinking can influence our health and well-being. The more powerful the positive thought processes are, the healthier we have the potential to be. Science and the medical profession now concede from research and evidence that when life is feeling good and we are happier, we enjoy good health. On the other hand, when life turns sour and we find ourselves burdened with worries, financial or otherwise, our bodies defence, our immune system, is compromised leaving us open and vulnerable to illness and disease. We know from experience that a compassionate loving heart, human contact, a gentle touch, or word can carry huge healing energy. The opposite is also true, and harsh words or actions can injure us inwardly. All sentient creatures are susceptible to positive and negative energy: a positive, caring, and loving attitude can work wonders.

Years ago, when I was a young mum, I worked briefly as a carer for abused children. It was my job to care for these children in a daily capacity while social services were building up a case for prosecution against the suspected abuser. It was amazing to watch how these children turned about from being scratchy, tearful, woeful looking tykes to beaming little monsters with the right diet, the right attention, big hugs, and lots of TLC. We all know how easily we forget our woes and troubles when life suddenly becomes happier our Spirit is lifted, and when our Spirit is lifted, so too is our well-being. But children are not the only ones who respond to Spiritual healing, animals do as well. All my life I have been rescuing abandoned animals who have been subjected to cruelty or neglect. These animals have turned up on my doorstep out of desperation for food and shelter, but nevertheless still very wary of human contact. Some of them have been at death's door. Sometimes veterinary help would suggest that nothing could be done, and it would be better to have the victim put to sleep. But Spiritual healing intervened. Prayers to the Angels and the Spirit world for help, along with a warm bed, dietary needs met, gentle words and a caring attitude and a great deal of TLC brought its own rewards. Over the years, I have seen the results of such intervention that has given new life to all sorts of animals, from chickens, ducks, and guinea pigs, to goats, horses, hedgehogs, and wild birds, not to mention numerous cats and dogs. Untainted by human conditioning, animals respond to the subjective properties of Spiritual healing which has been shown to come in many forms. It could be argued, of course, that in some cases veterinary treatment saved the day. However, the power of our actions and words should not be dismissed too quickly. Recent medical research of the placebo effect on back problems found that patients fared much better when receiving caring attention from their doctors even though they were given placebo medication as against patients who were given orthodox medication while receiving less attention. Research found that it wasn't just about the medication per se, it was about the length of time doctors spent with their patient, and how the patient responded thereof triggering the release of endorphins, natural painkillers that are similar in structure to morphine. {BBC 2 Horizon 4th October 2018 trials conducted by Dr Michael Mosley}

There have always been those practitioners of the healing arts who deliberately use these energies, or at least recognize them. A Spiritual healer believes in the premise that we are more Spirit than physical. They follow the belief and theory that everything on planet Earth is energy, extending out into the universe, the core of which is Spirit. To put it another way, it is our Life Force, an energy linked into the energy of all Life Forms all of which originate from the same source of all beginnings, a Universal energy, a Super Consciousness, a Creative Force, God if you prefer of all creation. I find that many people do not understand what is meant by Spirit, and so fail in the recognition of this beautiful phenomena. Instead, they consider it an old-fashioned, fringe concept. Yet many of us at some point in our lives may have experienced and felt a sudden elevation of our "Spirit", the elevation of our Life Force. For example, when we feel happy, the world around us can feel right, whether it is or not, giving us a tremendous sense of wellbeing and ease. Spiritual healing is thus about elevating our Life Force, stimulating its energy, a Spiritual component bringing harmony to disharmony. It is about bringing balance to the imbalance of the body's needs and welfare that creates dis-ease. It could be said that Spiritual healing gets to the "core of the matter" producing a rippling effect of well-being throughout the entire body. As opposed to just treating the symptoms like orthodox medicine and practitioners do, healing via the Spirit treats the whole person in a very holistic organic way.

Those with healing potential are usually extremely sensitive. There is no such thing as being "oversensitive", because anyone who wishes to become a healer should be able to "tune in" to the hidden energies around them, the celestial healing energies of Spirit and the Universal Force. They should be able to be "attuned" to those in need of the healing energies, for example the massage therapist who can intuitively seek out muscle tension, or the psychiatrist who can sense a patient's fear or anger. There are many ways in which this potential may become manifest - for some, the healing potential awakens and develops over time, whereas for others, the healing potential may awaken overnight at a turning point following a life-changing traumatic event. Either way, compassion, caring, and sympathetic awareness grows from a personal understanding that earthly life is short and tender, and that human beings and other sentient creatures, and planet Earth itself, are not infallible. The healing potential forms an awareness of Spirit through personal experiences and awakens the knowledge that all life is precious. There is often an urge to reach out for those less fortunate, perhaps victims of their own mental, emotional, or psychological urges, or the negative urges of others. For some people, the healing potential is a "gift" often inherited from previous generations. However, not everybody is attuned for it, and so do not have what it takes for ongoing healing development. True Healing potential requires us to be born with this innate characteristic for it to develop and be drawn out, and when the healing potential is there, ongoing Spiritual development is essential along with an appreciation and respect for Spirit.

The qualities and character we might expect from a healer are myriad. Obviously, a connection in some way to Spirit, and in that way often an appreciation of silence, solitude, and meditative practices. Meditation can come in many forms – physical through Yoga or other exercise, visual through artistic media, or auditory through the creation and appreciation of music. But conversely to Heal they must be willing and able to seek out and connect with other people – and in some sense this is a form of self-sacrifice. The recognition of dis-ease in other living creatures is enough to motivate them to help. Compassion, empathy, and tolerance of the fallibility of the human condition are therefore innate to them, perhaps as qualities that they were born with, or perhaps awakened after particular experiences. The healer thus is someone who has been on a long journey towards self: assessing, learning, and teaching along the way, demonstrating that learning and teaching is a perfect circle. The healer must be dedicated to improving their Spiritual awareness, that all life is energy and Spirit – because the more aware they are of this connection, the more effective they will be.

It should be clear that in many cases the healer does not heal per se, but often reaches out with healing energy in their heart, allowing a rippling effect to take hold in the wider community. The ability to link into the healing energies of the Universal Spirit can be found in many forms. For example, some people seem able to connect with the living forces of plant life through their "green fingers." They seem to have the Midas touch when it comes to gardening or working on the land. Other people are said to have "healing hands" as it is found that all sentient life responds to their human touch and kindness. Some people have a unique caring way when dealing with those less fortunate, whether Homo sapiens or other species of animal. Some people make excellent doctors and nurses, carers or veterinary surgeons or charity workers. They just seem to have a natural knack in their professional life. And there are those that "care" in their daily lives who often go unrecognized. Thus, we can see, the notion of Spiritual healing can be found without anyone ever giving it much thought. Furthermore, the way the healer manifests their ability may differ.

Having inherited the gift of Spiritual healing I believe from lifelong experience in its power. So, in recognition of the Universal energies around me I always begin a healing session by quietly saying a prayer to myself. It goes like this; "I call upon the Archangels and the Holy Spirit, and I call upon the Spiritual healing workforce to please come forward and assist me in this program of healing." This is followed by quietly going into a meditative state, a light trance as it were, where the healing medium is said to be "overshadowed" by the healing energies of the Spirit world while remaining fully aware of what they are doing and what others are saying around them. This state of semi-trance happens when the medium feels a sense of detachment, a sleep like condition as if viewing things through a haze. Nevertheless, I can still influence what takes place around me and return to a normal stage of consciousness very quickly. However, sometimes I can go into a deep trance, feeling at one with Spirit, resulting from a complete trust which has developed over many years. Healing mediumship might involve several states of altered consciousness according to the medium's individual Spiritual development, skill, and progression.

With Contact healing or Near-to-the-Body healing, the healing influences of Spirit rely on the healer becoming "connected" to the patient through the vehicle of touch or near-touch. In all cases of Spiritual healing, the healer is guided by the Spiritual forces and the Spiritual energies to the areas of the patient's body where the healing energies are needed the most. The healer, as a human being must develop and evolve Spiritually before they can become attuned to the healing energies of Spirit from the Spirit world while remaining utterly passive to human urges and the mundane world around them. It could be said, the healer has to "give" of themselves to the Spiritual world which in turn "gives" to other life in earthly form hence the phrase, "from Spirit, through Spirit, to Spirit. Or put another way, a blending of Souls. I would argue that as we grow Spiritually, so too does the power of positive thought. For example, Distance healing involves the capacity to send healing thoughts/prays to someone that might be in the same room. Whereas Absent healing can be projected to many people at once anywhere in the world. Both types rely on thought or prayer, the healing influences of Spirit to work through the healer's telepathic faculty or the ability to go into a meditative state that relies on focus and deep concentration. In other words, the more powerful the psychic/intuitive/telepathic faculty is, along with a positive faith in the healing goodness of a creative force and the administrators of a Spiritual world, the more powerful the thought and prayer processes are likely to be. It should be said however, that neither Absent nor Distance healing relies on faith alone, therefore is not the same as Faith healing. In all aspects of Spiritual healing, the healer always acts as an intermediary for Spirit from the Spiritual world to the patient's Spirit hence its title, "Spiritual Healing" and the phrase, "from Spirit, through Spirit, to Spirit".

There is another form of healing known as Magnetic healing which relies on the notion that the Universal energy or Life Force permeates all creation on planet Earth and all-around the different manifestations of this Life Force, including the Earth itself is an electromagnetic energy field. This energy field, referred to by Spiritualists as the Aura can be seen in various hues of colour or tuned into or sensed by a highly "gifted" Spiritual healer/medium. The energy of the inner Life Force can be replenished with food and drink, helping with the replenishment of the outer energy field or Aura, which is also helped by the absorption of cosmic radiation. Thus, Magnetic healing is a combination of the healer's Life Force energy and the energy of the electromagnetic energy field, the Aura. The vital bodily energy of the healer, who may have it in abundance, is transferred to the patient who may be depleted of it. This transfer of vital bodily energy arises in the initial stages of healing when the healer has established a link or rapport with the patient but has failed to sever that link when the Spiritual energies takeover. This usually happens when the Spiritual healer has become involved with the patient, either on a mental or emotional or psychological level. Of course, a link or rapport of attunement with the client/patient is vital at the beginning of a Spiritual healing session. But equally important, is for the healer to recognize when to stem the flow of their own vital energy, becoming a passive instrument or conduit for the Spiritual healing workforce, enabling their energies of healing to take over. In other words, Magnetic healing is not Spiritual healing at all, but arises when the healer has given too much of themselves, leaving both them and later, their client depleted of energy and potentially feeling a lot worse.

No matter how we choose to heal, whether through a touch, a cuddle, a kind word, or action, we will be acting as go-between for the healing energies of the Spirit world, stimulating and igniting the Spirit of those we care about. So how do the healing influences work through a Spiritual healer? Many times, the healer is asked,

"If Spirit can heal, then why can't we all just ask the Spirit world to heal everyone who is sick?"

"Couldn't we then eliminate the need for a medical profession and Spiritual healers?"

These are profound questions, as indeed is the answer. When I asked my own Spirit guides for answers, this is what came through: In the Spirit world, that is perfect, disease and sickness no longer exist thus a medical profession is not required. It is the purity of Spirit and the Spirit world and the healing energies of our original source, the Creative Life Force or Universal Energy or Spirit, or God where the healing energies exist. However, in our earthly existence, where Man is still governed by his own mental, emotional, physical, or psychological urges, we will always be subjected to our own inner negative urges, and the inner negative urges of other people. These influences can lead to imbalance within our psyche and physical bodies which provide fertile ground for sickness and disease. The Spiritual healer, as a human being, is also not infallible. They are still available to negative, destructive urges which in turn can put their health at risk, but as someone who was born with the "gift" of attuning to Spirit and the potential for mediumship or healing ability, the healer can avail themselves of becoming a passive instrument for the channelling of healing energies of Spirit. As a human being, the Spiritual healer does not heal per se. They simply act as a Spiritual intermediary or a conduit for Spirit from the Spiritual world, which will in turn stimulate or activate the patient's Spirit, lifting it to greater heights enabling the patient's body to heal itself.

Not every human being has the “gift” of attuning to the Spiritual world, nor will Spirit heal except on invitation. The recipient of healing must be responsive whether consciously or subconsciously. Not all life on planet Earth responds to Spiritual healing because not all life on planet Earth seeks to be healed or for that matter, wants to be healed! The celestial realm does not interfere with the stimuli or free will of the earthly form. Hence, the Spirit world cannot eliminate sickness and disease here on earth any more than the Spirit world can eliminate the multitudes of different negative urges attributed to human/sentient behaviour that create sickness and disease. Hence, the healing influences that work through Spirit rely on the “gifted” individual who can relay the healing energies of Spirit to those that request it either consciously or subconsciously. In other words, there must be a "will” to get well again. A spark that ignites the Spirit to survive, to live, a willing or responsive recipient, the healer being the transmitter, the patient being the receiver.

So, does Spiritual healing ever fail? Again, this is a profound question and to answer it we first must establish what do we mean by Spiritual healing? We have already shown that the first premise of Spiritualism is that Man is Spirit as opposed to physical and its Man’s Spiritual self that uniquely connects us to each other and to other Life forms which in turn are all linked into the Greater Universal Energy, the Universal Spirit, the Creative Life Force. So, when we talk about Spiritual healing, we are referring to the healing energies of the Spiritual component of those we wish to heal and of the Creative Universal Force and the ability to link into that energy. Because we are all uniquely different from each other, it follows that some of us could be susceptible to inherited health problems while other people are more susceptible to the Law of Consequences which is the outcome of cause and effect, a process of Natural Law. Hence, the Spirit world cannot eliminate sickness and disease here on earth, any more than the Spirit world or (orthodox medicine!) can eliminate the multitudes of different negative urges attributed to sentient behaviour. So, to answer our question "does Spiritual healing ever fail?" The answer is yes, it does sometimes. But mostly it works in wondrous miraculous ways that go unrecognized as such in our daily lives.

Can it be then we are all healers at heart? Well, it could be argued, yes to a certain extent. It depends on the innate characteristics with which we are born. Healing potential thus lies within some of us, but not necessarily all. Some human beings are selfish, inconsiderate, or destructive creatures, directed by their own negative energies born of the Ego. Others are guided by their Spirit and have an innately healing persona. To have a natural healing ability rest on the availability of a caring, compassionate energy force. Not everyone has the same capabilities, but that is no reason why we should not all try. We are all on a personal journey while living here on earth with lessons to learn, developing Spiritual wisdom accordingly. So, how can we be self-healing? The answer is, to become healers in our own right. To take control of our own bodies, our actions, our thoughts, our lives. If, as science and human experience has shown us, our mental attitudes can positively and negatively affect our physical health, we can surely make a move to heal ourselves through improving our thoughts, and through them our connection to Spirit? In the same way as we can and should limit the physical stressors on our body, such as pollution, poor diet, smoking, poor sleep and excessive alcohol and caffeine consumption, it should be clear to the reader now that the mental stressors should also be addressed to strengthen our Spirit. Our psychic stressors are in many ways though those of our own making – they are not a direct response to an external pressure, but rather our internal interpretation of them, and therefore are susceptible to our control. As we can train our bodies to become stronger, more flexible, faster – so too can we train our thoughts to swing towards positivity, self-encouragement, self-worth and to find joy and beauty in the world. Mindfulness and meditation, whether led by a guide or self-directed, can be enormously beneficial, and have been associated for millennia with a deeper Spiritual connection. There are many ways to improve our mental well-being, whether through creating art, connecting with nature, giving service to the needy, or finding like-minded souls to share experiences and time with. And once we are in control of our thought processes, whether we choose it through the process of physical exercise, joining a club or volunteering, yoga, meditation, mindfulness, or complimentary therapies, we are on the road to developing the ability to focus on positiveness as against negativity, submerging the Ego, allowing the Spirit to come to the fore. For positivity is attuned to Spirit, and Spirit only works for the betterment of self and the world around. And when we feel healed within and the world is right, healed around us, the Spirit is "lifted." Of course, some people would argue that positivity could be felt from the outcome of an evil act born of the Ego, and it is true. But this type of positivity born of the Ego does not touch the Soul, the Spirit, it does not "lift" it. Hence there is no healing energy from this experience, and it is often transient and short-lived. This negative energy is detrimental to the self and the world at large. Healing energy only comes about from positive thought processes born of the Spirit. In other words, when we have love, compassion, humility, and a caring attitude in our hearts born of the Spirit, our healing capacity can be enormously powerful indeed. We all have the capacity to heal ourselves and the world at large depending on our own personal Spiritual development.

The benefits of a positive mindset are legion: we know it is possible, look around. We hear of people escaping war, losing their homes, their livelihoods and loved ones, escaping to other lands to start again, and making a success of themselves. We hear of people born into poverty only to make an enormous success of their lives, bringing them not only financial security, but also emotional fulfilment. We read in magazines and newspapers the results of a slimmer who has shed pounds by sheer determined thought processes. When we channel our thoughts through the vehicle of positive determination the outcome can be spectacular, as we have seen in the Paralympics or Prof Stephen Hawking. Disabilities have proved no obstacle with positive thought processes. We hear of people climbing mountains, sailing the oceans solo, walking to the North Pole, all showing positive, determined thought processes. We know it is possible to overcome huge disabilities or disadvantages whether of a financial or social or cultural or physical or mental nature. We know that positive thought processes can overcome great challenges as well as help to strengthen our immune systems, helping to combat illness and disease reminding us once again of René Descartes' philosophy, "I think, therefore I am".

Chapter 8

The Law of Attraction

Over my lifetime I have made some particularly good friendships. Some of these friendships have lasted many years, some not so long. Others have petered out over the years as my own interests, opinions and attitudes have changed. This has probably come about mainly because I have moved to a new house, district, or country many times. This has ensured new experiences and opportunities being presented to me leaving promises to stay in touch forgotten in the mire of new beginnings. Life is different now of course, with Internet social networking. When I was a child, my parents were constantly moving to a new house, either within the confines of the West Country of England or to Australia and back again. My mother once worked out that she had moved to a new house every 2 ½ years during the first forty odd years of her life. Consequently, moving to a new house has never fazed me. Having inherited my parent's wanderlust, I have lived in many parts of the British Isles including Scotland and Southern Ireland. Accordingly, my friendships have developed in relation to the experiences I have had and the environments in which I have lived. What has intrigued me, looking back in hindsight, is that I can see that my friendships have had the same experiences as me, they have matched my psychological, emotional and/or mental development at the time of our friendship. For example, my early friendships were formed through my working environments when I worked in a drawing office. Later when I had young children, I started to form friendships with other parents through school environments. When I was going through emotional trauma of divorce or bereavement, I seemed to attract like-minded friendships, people that were going through the same experiences or had been through the same. One of my friends had also married her first cousin {the same as me}. She also had a great love of animals and believed in the benefits of holistic healthcare and saw no reason why it should not complement orthodox practice. {The same as me.} She once confided in me that despite being a member of a close family, she always felt on the fringe because other members of their circle had very different opinions and attitudes from hers. {The same as me.} Later in life, I made friends with a woman who also had had two nervous breakdowns on the back of two painful divorces and she also had had an abusive mother and been ostracised in later life. {The same as me.} The interesting thing is, that none of my friendships had known anything about me nor I of them until after we had met and got to know each other. Yet as complete strangers, we had been drawn to each other as if by instinct. Even young children will form close bonds with other children, while keeping their distance from others.

It certainly does seem that we are drawn to people that come from the same background as us, the same culture, the same social level, where the same attitudes and opinions prevail. Mostly we do not realise we are doing it. It is not necessarily something we do deliberately and consciously. But somehow, we can home-in on people we share common experiences or interests with. It is as if we all have antennae tuned into higher frequencies that enable us to connect with like-minded people. These attractions are born of our subconscious, our psychic tendencies. These help us to identify people who we automatically feel comfortable with, people who we share common denominators with, people who have had the same life experiences as ourselves. Here we are reminded of the old axiom,

"Birds of a feather flock together".

Thus, our friendships are likely to be people who usually come from the same social background as ourselves, people who share the same social interests such as in sport, religion, philosophies, attitudes and opinions or hobbies and suchlike. As with many other people, most of my adult friendships have been formed through my employment environment. It has been found that many people meet their lifelong partner within their working environment or perhaps through some social activity or network. Today it is not uncommon for friendships to be formed or couples to meet each other through computer networking sites. Here people can identify a potential partner in the comfort of one's home by simply reading their personal profile. Other couples meet each other while studying at the same college or university. It fascinates me to observe that a sport will attract a particular type of person. For example, some people enjoy physical activity either to participate and/or as a spectator. Some will enjoy indoor activities, while others prefer to be outside. Some people enjoy water activities, while others enjoy activities associated with the countryside and/or with animals. On the other hand, there are those people who are attracted to the sunny climates preferring to relax and sunbathe. Other people are adventurous and like a challenge, while other people prefer to go binge drinking every weekend! There are people who enjoy a night at the ballet or the opera or theatre, and people who enjoy a quiet night in with a cup of cocoa perhaps listening to classical music. There are people who like to be noisy and rowdy, turning every event into a party. And there are those who enjoy a quiet night in, a good soak in the bath, perhaps an evening of yoga and meditation. There are people who enjoy a good social life, or belonging to a club, and there are those who would like to be alone.

In a career capacity, once again we find “Birds of a feather flock in together". There are those people with a pedantic nature, articulate in their mental thinking attracted to employment in an office environment perhaps ambitious for management, banking, and suchlike. There are those who are articulate in craftsmanship skills more suitable for intricate manual work. And there are those with academic leanings most often found in teaching professions or perhaps in the medical profession or something similar. There are those who are proficient at using their brain, and those who are proficient at using their hands. There are those who enjoy working inside, and those who prefer working outdoors. There are those who prefer working in a large organisation perhaps drawn to the Armed Forces seeking challenge and perhaps foreign travel, and those who seek to care for others. And those who prefer being self-employed. Whatever our forte in career aspirations, our innate attributes are drawn to and used in careers as befitting our characters and personalities. Consequently, we are not all doctors, teachers, members of the Armed Forces, shopkeepers, scientists, gardeners, joiners, or members of the police force etc. We are all different, each of us unique from our own mould, yet having something within us that attracts us to something that is within other people as well. When we observe the behaviour and nature of those around us, we can identify that the human population is attracted to and enjoys belonging to its own “tribe” in accordance with one’s innate attributes, personality, emotional, mental and/or psychological development. The human population thus appears to be tribal in a career capacity, in emotional relationships and in social activity. We have only to observe the vast numbers of people that follow a sport such as football, cricket, or tennis to notice the tribal influence within the human psyche. People are always drawn to a tribe of similar ilk. Thus, we can observe one of the workings of

"The Law of Attraction".

As our personalities develop over our lifetime, we find changing interests, attitudes and opinions give rise to changing priorities. And it is these changing priorities that have a rippling effect attracting like-minded people into our life. From our life experiences, old habits, opinions, and attitudes fall away. These in addition often mean old friendships and relationships that once may have seemed important also begin to fall away as new friendships come into our life to meet the demands of the new you. Attitudes towards personal relationships change as our feelings, emotions and opinions alter in accordance with our life experiences. Even close family members can drift apart as they find they no longer share common ground. Thus, we can still feel isolated even within a family. It is not always easy to act in accordance with the changes that have occurred within us. We may feel guilty or uncomfortable when we realise, we no longer have anything in common with old friendships or personal relationships. However, no matter how difficult we may find the task, it is always best to be honest with oneself and with others around us. To live in the shadow of other people's expectations is to stifle one's own emotional, mental, or psychological thus Spiritual development. It is important to remember that these inner changes are natural shifts for all of us. These changes are transforming, they are a natural part of our development as we travel our Life Path attempting to enrich our Soul. We are not all the same, we come from different moulds with different lessons to learn and different destinies to meet. Thus, many people will undergo many changes in their life, others less so. Some people are born to stagnate and vegetate. But for many of us as we grow older, we begin to observe that the many things we found important when we were younger no longer constitute a place on our priority list. This shows that our changing personal relationships and/or friendships and acquaintances have shifted to a higher frequency as our development becomes more Spiritually based.

Another side to the Law of Attraction is the theory that we have the mental capacity to attract good things into our life, that by focusing upon positive thoughts we can bring about positive results. Equally, the opposite is said to be true, if we focus upon negative thoughts, we may expect negative results. In other words, the Law of Attraction espouses the theory that we hold the power of choice. This theory is taken from the premise that we are all in our present position because of our past thoughts. Therefore, it follows that we have the mental power to control our future. There have been many books and journals espousing similar principles that if we focus long and hard enough upon the physical form of our goal, we may become rich or famous or anything else we are wishing and reaching for. The Law of Attraction at this level thus suggests that the mind through focus and/or observation has the capacity to cause collapse or affect reality directly, thus suggesting the ability of quantum mysticism. Can this be true you may well ask yourself? If it is so, then all we must do is write a wish list and concentrate long and hard enough on the objects of our desire. But this theory would also suggest that those that suffer from negative experiences in life have really got what they deserve, because they just were not positive enough in their thinking! It all sounds a bit too simplistic, doesn't it? Even hard-hearted for those less fortunate. The success of the film "The Secret" {2006} demonstrates how most people would really like to believe that something good could happen in their life if they remain positive and that maybe they really do have free will and can exercise it. But critics of this film and book point out that if the universe can manifest abundance by mere thought, why does poverty, homelessness and starvation still prevail not only in the Third

World but in the Western world as well. And what about those people who die under dreadful circumstances such as in a car or plane crash or as a victim of war or murder? It could be argued thus that critics of positive thinking have a point. After all, people do not deliberately seek out negative situations to make themselves miserable, or to put their lives at risk, or do they? And if there are an abundance of people who pray and send out positive affirmations for the benefit of those less fortunate, why is there still too much suffering in the world (and why hasn't my husband won the lottery yet!)? These are valid questions. Perhaps I should leave you to answer these questions after you have read what the Spiritual realm has informed me.

Messages come to me all the time from the Spiritual realm: sometimes personal or related to mundane subjects of more worldly events. They usually come to me from someone residing on the "other side" accompanied with a visitation of who the messenger is. Sometimes I know them, other times I do not. Sometimes I "hear" messages without knowing who has spoken. Other times I just seem to know things without knowing how I have come to know. Regarding this topic, this was one of those occasions of the latter.

Through the Natural Laws of Cause and Effect -Reaction and Consequences which are determined by our innate persona of emotional, mental, physical, and Spiritual traits that make-up our psychological characteristics we are born with a particular life pattern that determines our life journey. All Life is affected by natural laws. We are affected by natural laws which we only cease at the end of our lives when we have learnt the lessons we came here to learn, thus fulfilling our life purpose and enriching our Soul. If our Soul is not enriched in this lifetime we may go around again into another life until we have reached the highest level of Spiritual attainment. There are many lessons to learn over many lifetimes until we are at One with the Universal Energy or Spirit. Only then can our Soul be truly Enriched. Thus, we come to this life at different levels of Spiritual development which we have inherited from previous lives. {For me, I have inherited traits from two great aunts who were Spiritual mediums.} These inherited attitudes and traits constitute a mixture of negative and positive thinking of which most of us will have a balance of each. However, some people will be born into negative situations in accordance with the Law of Cause and Effect from a previous lifetime or be urged to unleash negativity through their current thought processes and actions in this life. Positive thinking is not just a matter of "wishful thinking" but involves having high levels of perseverance, endurance, the courage of one's convictions and an awful lot of faith and confidence in one's own abilities and in the notion of a magnanimous universe. Not everyone will be born with these additional qualities and attributes that make positive thinking a long-term prospect. It is not enough to simply have a vivid imagination giving access to a parallel world. Imagination affords us access into parallel worlds that may or may not be available to us in accordance with our life purpose here in this life. For example, you may imagine yourself to be a famous singer or have ambitions to be an astute successful businessperson but unless your innate characteristics and life lessons and purpose dictate that positive outcome, it is unlikely to happen. Many people have dreams for a better lifestyle that go beyond their own innate capabilities to achieve. We may thus attract good things into our life by exerting positive thoughts, but we can only do so if it is in our character to do so and is part of our life lessons and life purpose in this lifetime. In addition, we should also consider that good things may happen in our life because of positive thinking but can only come to fruition at a particular time in our life. It is about the Law of Synchronicity and how everything else needs to be in place before certain things can happen. Thus, we may attract good things into our life by positive thinking, but these good things may only come about after many years of demanding work and perseverance.

Observation of our astrology analyses can help identify our potential positive and negative traits and the areas of our life in which it is likely to affect us. For example, we may have positive traits that affect our relationships, but negative traits that affect our career or health. Analysis of our astrological progressions has the potential to identify more fortuitous times or not as the case may be. By understanding ourselves and perhaps addressing our negative traits we can attempt to improve our personas and develop as individuals. At the same time, this learning process can be found in the experiences our innate characteristics urge us to take. For example, a young active man or young woman may have an adventurous streak in them. They may long to broaden their horizons through global travel and experience different people and cultures. They may enjoy taking risks. They may be patriotic and like the idea of serving their country. These innate traits in their characters may thus urge them to join one of the Armed Forces where being injured or even killed would be an occupational hazard. So, despite being positive and upbeat and expecting the best in life our hypothetical young man or woman through their innate traits and characteristics urge them to join a tribe that put their lives at risk. In this sense, they are acting in accordance with the Law of Attraction, which produces a particular Life Path. But whether they are killed or injured is determined by their Law of Cause and Effect and the lessons they have come to this life to learn. Many people survive experiences of negativity, which sets them down on a different path in life: a path of higher understanding and Spirituality. It is as if their lessons in this lifetime are to experience and survive severe challenges.

So how can this be? What makes us all so different, so unique, following different Life Paths? The answer lies in the universe, which is governed and abides by many Natural Laws. For example, as well as the Law of attraction and the Law of synchronicity and Cause and Effect, there are the Laws of Reaction, Consequences, Gravity, Time, and the Laws of Motion. These laws can work alone, but mostly they work in conjunction with each other, thus ensuring a natural time and place and action for everything that happens. These laws affect us as individuals, as tribes, as a mass, as countries, including planet Earth as an organic structure. These laws affect the psychological, emotional, mental, and Spiritual development of the individual or Carl Jung's "collective unconscious." And so, under the illusion of Man-Made chaos there is always Divine reason and order which teaches us to "go with the flow." The Law of Attraction and the Law of Cause and Effect always work in conjunction with each other. We are all affected by the Law of Cause and Effect in accordance with our deeds, thoughts and actions when residing in a past life or while in this life. In other words, our actions will always have a reaction. This ensures that we are all at different stages in our life, emotionally, mentally, physically, and spiritually. We are not all destined to be rich or famous. Nor are we all destined to live or work on the dark side of life. Most of us are destined to take a middle road. But whatever road we are on, we can be sure it is in accordance with our ongoing spiritual development either within this lifetime or from a previous life. Throughout our lives, as our development unfolds, we gravitate or are pulled in a direction towards specific people, events, or situations. So, no matter how hard we focus on our wish list in a positive way, for many of us it is unlikely to happen. But that is not to say we should not remain positive in our thinking, for as we learned earlier, people that take a cheerful outlook are more likely to be healthier in both mind and body. Positive attributes and attitudes can and do manifest positive results, and negative attributes and attitudes bringing the opposite. We can thus improve our circumstances by taking positive action and holding a positive view of life.

When my husband and I became financially embarrassed, we eased our worry and stress by taking long walks on the beach or in the countryside. A brisk walk no matter where you live, preferably away from traffic and other polluted areas, can help to alleviate stress levels - breathing fresh air and energy into the body. Being out in a natural environment can help put your worries and concerns into perspective and often brings creative solutions to mind. In addition, my husband and I became acquainted with a lot of people while out on our walks. Through light-hearted chitchat our Spirits were lifted, and firmer friendships made. In the autumn, when the hedgerows were splendid with edible fruits and flowers, we would pick these to make home-made jam and wine. For the price of a few bags of sugar we were able to replenish our larder with nature's luxury goods. Both my husband and I have been blessed with down-to-earth traditional cookery skills. Our table is always full both for ourselves and when we are entertaining socially. We may have been paupers at times, but we always dine like royalty! By taking a cheerful outlook and positive actions, my husband and I can attract good things into our life.

The Law of Attraction works at a macro and micro level in conjunction with other universal laws. At a macro level, we can use the Law of Attraction through our prayers and affirmations to tap into "the collective unconscious". At this level, our thought processes benefit the world at large in accordance with individual journeys. We are not all here to have the same experiences or to take the same view of the world. By the end of our lives, we will all have a different worldview. Nevertheless, at a micro level we can use the Law of Attraction by focusing upon positive thought processes to improve our attitudes and behaviour which would have a rippling effect on our personal circumstances. Positive thinking could thus improve our lives, for example, we might become more content with less, and so become more Spiritually attuned. However, positive thinking will not necessarily save us from a health challenge or a premature death. It will not necessarily save us from being killed in an accident or being a victim of abuse, murder, or war. Life is full of challenges, highs, and lows, it's not perfect, it wasn't designed to be! We are one of many we share this planet with. On the other hand, however, positive thinking can and does improve the condition of our health, our mental and emotional wellbeing, the wellbeing of the Soul. The power of the Law of Attraction is real. When we recognise this, and come to understand its implications, by using positive affirmations we can improve our lot in life and help to improve the life of others in accordance with their life lessons and life purpose on Planet Earth. We are all individuals, but at the same time, "No Man is an Island!"

Chapter 9

Soulmate

It has taken me half a lifetime to find a relationship I feel comfortable with. A relationship where I have been able to be myself without fear of punishment, judgement, and discrimination. It goes back to my challenging relationship with my mother. She was an extremely negative person, always attempting to impose her will, opinions, attitudes, and judgements onto other people. And if you did not live up to her notions or conform to them, she considered you disloyal - which would then justify (in her mind) her judgements and punishments. For me, as a strong-willed child and guided by Spirit, this meant a lifetime of periodical abuse, mostly emotional and mental, with the occasional physical attack just to get her point of view across. Her violent temper was only exposed behind closed doors, typical characteristics of an abusive person. She was a small woman with a tongue as sharp as barbed wire. I have seen intelligent grown men of authority reduced to a nervous wreck because of getting on the wrong side of her! Consequently, very few people would risk exposing their true selves, let alone their true opinions in front of her. This was true of all of those who came to know her, and was especially true of her family, her husband, and her children. She kept us down, she would put us in our place by undermining our confidence with her derogatory, demeaning remarks. As with a lot of abusers, my mother's drive was a discontented jealous heart, urging her to feel threatened by other people's happiness or successes. This challenging foundation in my early life has meant that for the first 40 years I did not have the confidence to reveal my true self, the true nature of who I really am within my relationships. There have been people I was close to emotionally or mentally: people such as my dad, my brother, my grandparents and some aunts and uncles, people I loved very much and could trust, but when it came to more intimate relationships, I did not have the confidence to reveal my true self until I met my third husband. I am not complaining though- I have come to realize and understand this is my journey, my reasons for being here, my lessons to learn thereof in this lifetime. My redeeming feature has always been from early childhood my blessing to be psychic, telepathic, intuitive, and sensitive to the hidden energies around me. This acute sensitivity has enabled me to tune in to "another world" and be guided by Spirit: Spirit from the "other side," or Spirit within. But listening to Spirit does not necessarily ensure harmony or a peaceful life, for sometimes Spirit is contrary to what others have in mind, what is Truth and what is best. Thus, Spirit is always in conflict with Ego, Ego within the self and Ego within others which impacts and persuades our free will.

With over seven billion people now living on planet Earth, foreign travel and access through the Internet, the plethora of relationships now available to us would seem enormous. I remember as a young teenager, after the breakup with a boyfriend, my friends would say, "Don't worry, there are plenty more fish in the sea". But is this true? We all know, or at least most of us will come to know, that despite all the people we come to meet or interface with over our lifetime, there are only a few that we feel a strong attraction to or have a strong affinity with. And so, I have come to understand that the Law of Attraction is in place as a guiding light, stimulating our Spirit, our Soul which tugs at our solar plexus, informing us when the moment is right to change direction, to be drawn to a particular relationship. This is different from following the Ego which only urges for material wealth or sexual gratification. Our task on earth is to come to learn the difference between the Ego and the Spirit and in doing so, we will come to recognize our soulmate. So, what do we mean by soulmate? In modern secular usage, it most often refers to a romantic partner related to the concept of love where one can achieve the strongest bond with another person, where one can feel complete. A cynic might argue that it is an ideal that is hard to achieve, explaining why so many couples today end their relationship in the divorce courts. On the other hand, as Spiritualist, I would say, perhaps it is an indicator that we are all on a road searching for our soulmate.

When I look back over my own life, I can see that my reasons for marrying my three husbands were each quite different. Each time I was at a different stage and development in my life, therefore the urges and reasons for marrying were also vastly different. On the back of emotional insecurities, having left home at the age of eighteen because of my mum, I was only a month away from celebrating my 20th birthday when I married for the first time. It wasn't just physical attraction or his sense of humour that drew me to him, but instinct that hit my solar plexus that informed me this man was right for me and would be the father to my children. Instinct and a Spiritual message from my grandfather many years previously had informed me I would marry a Cornishman. Thus, I knew intuitively, this Cornishman and his family represented emotional security at a time in my life when my own immediate family, headed by my mother, represented a fractured emotional bond. This marriage lasted 17 years, encompassing difficulties like all relationships, but ended as it was destined to end, on the back of challenging times, so challenging that it weakened my resolve to continue the relationship. It led to a nervous breakdown. I had always known in my heart that my relationship with my first husband was not destined to last till death us do part. We were incredibly young when we married and over the years we had grown apart. The challenges had seen to that. When it came to divorce, instinct and Spirit informed me, the moment was right to move on.

Unlike my first marriage, I ignored my instincts, my Spirit within, when I married for the second time. And married instead on the back of my Ego, flamed by a mixture of financial insecurity and lack of confidence born of my previous divorce which was not helped by my parent's negative attitude which made me feel even more worthless. As a first cousin, my second husband provided a sense of emotional security born out of years of perceived familiarity. There was a sense that we "knew" each other even when in fact, we hardly knew each other at all having spent extraordinarily little time together over the years. Having spent all his working life as a highly paid officer in a foreign merchant Navy, in the days when foreign travel was only available for the privileged few, he not only provided financial security, but instilled a romantic view of him, not only by me, but the whole family. And so, at a time when I was vulnerable, I was drawn into the relationship for all the wrong reasons and an idealistic notion of him which was far from the truth. Looking at him through rose tinted glasses, the relationship was not born to last and so fragile in its sensitivities that when the truth came out it was soon broken. Having been warned by the Spirit of my grandfather that this marriage would only last three years, it indeed ended abruptly when I discovered this man had all the hallmarks of my mother! The horror of discovering his violent temper, that he had been in jail for violent assault, his aptitude to want control, along with his liking of pornography ensured my romantic view of him was soon dissolved. He could never look me in the eye, informing me, he does not like to reveal too much of himself, he is not what he seems! I learnt very quickly that his principles, attitudes, and opinions were antithesis to mine. And so, we can say that my second marriage was based on a romantic notion of love, and fed the perception I would have everything, including financial security. But when it came to providing freedom of expression, without fear, prejudice, or punishment thus encouraging my self-worth and confidence in myself, the characteristics of my second husband were attempting to do the opposite. Predisposed to react negatively to his controlling violent characteristics in the long-term, my Spirit, my Soul, knew instinctively his persona would only destroy and undermine my self-worth further. I guess you could say that my second marriage was a real learning curve, bringing home to me what really matters within my relationships.

On the back of encouragement from Spirit within, and Spirit from the "other world," I found employment at a local defence company. Here I met my third husband at a point in our lives when a crisis would unfold, a crisis that was so major and so wounding, it would change our lives forever. Both of us, having reached a zenith of the first half of our lives, were now about to see it all destroyed! Our Souls recognized in the other suitable travelling companions, each helping the other over the bumpy road that lay ahead. And so, my relationship with my third husband has been blessed ensuring 28 years of emotional and mental security and protection, enriching my Soul, and allowing me to grow. We seem to sing from the same song sheet. That is not to say, it has been a marriage made in heaven - far from it. The challenges that we have faced over the years have been harder than either of us have experienced before with previous partners. Yet this time round, these challenges have made us stronger, both as individuals and together. And over that time, love has developed and deepened, a love so deep and so strong it has given each of us confidence to expose our deepest fears and our wildest dreams. It has allowed each of us to become ourselves. We often feel, "it's us against the world". From the moment we met, we felt at ease with one another, communication has always been easy. We just seem to understand each other, we are mentally united, we have so much in common. We accept each other, flaws, and all. We do not always need to be sexually active we are simply happy to be in each other's company, ascribing at times to Plato's platonic love, enabling and stimulating our attention to be directed to Spiritual matters. Each of us have learnt through our relationship that there are other forces at work. Indeed, if it were not for my third husband, my Dermot, I wouldn't have had the courage to stand up and say, "I am a Spiritual medium and healer and I want to write." I have finally been encouraged to disclose my true self. There was a sense of déjà vu when we met - indeed we discovered to our utter amazement that we had been following each other around having worked, lived or visited the same places, only missing each other with a margin of several years - until in the end, when the moment was right, we met! We have no fear of expressing our deepest feelings even if it leads to intense rows. We can look each other in the eye, without fear of remorse, regret, or punishment. We seem to know instinctively the relationship will never break. Neither of us feel challenged or worried over the other's independence. This relationship enriches our Souls, and in keeping with Soulmates brings to the surface that which needs to be healed enabling each of us to become ourselves, to fulfil our destinies. To accomplish all our karmic tasks and lessons.

So, was I destined to have three marriages? If one believes in the theory and philosophy of astrology, then the answer is yes. There is certainly evidence in my natal astrology chart that I am likely to have more than one husband! I have learnt over my lifetime that I have been drawn to different relationships for varied reasons at various times in my life at distinct stages of my emotional, mental, or Spiritual development. I have learnt we are drawn to relationships in which we are meant to have children. I have learnt we are drawn to relationships that are only meant to be temporary, to close out a karmic chapter in our life to give us experiences and lessons thereof. I have learnt we are drawn to relationships that can be great supporters, perhaps a long-term companion, but which are limited in their capacity to enrich our Soul and Spirit. Some people may be lucky, they may be destined to find a life partner, a relationship based the true meaning of love where warts and all are accepted unconditionally. All our relationships and partnerships are there to provide experiences and lessons. It is about the Law of Attraction, the guiding light of our Soul which exudes only Love, our Spirit which matches us up with the very person we are meant to be with at a particular time in our life. So, in a sense, any of our close relationships can be soulmates, such as a sibling, parent, grandparent, or friend. But this does not mean the relationship will last forever, because we are always subject to our free will, and nor does it mean you will not come up against challenges, for where there is love, there is also pain. Soul relationships include both, but only Soul relationships have the capacity to work things through allowing us to become ourselves. Only through love and pain can unresolved issues come to the surface: the intimacy of Soul relationships brings life lessons to the surface. We all want a pain-free life, and pain free relationships, but challenges are not necessarily a dreadful thing. Challenges help us grow, they help us develop, they provide wisdom, they help us to take responsibility for who we are innately, paving the Path which we tread to express our free will. We all spend a lot of time questioning whether we are in the right relationship or not, and this occurs most frequently during periods of discord, pain and discomfort born of fear. But if we recognize that our pain, discomfort, and fear come from within ourselves, it becomes our personal challenge rather than that of the other person, and a clarion call to change!

So, how can we change? We can turn our feeling of fear into one of love. That is not to say we should stick around in an abusive relationship or tolerate relationships that undermine our self-worth, but what it does mean is that if we choose love, we can see people, including ourselves, beyond their mistakes. When we choose love, which is of the Soul, our Spirit, we can see the potential in our partner even when they do not see it themselves. When we listen to our innate gut feelings, our intuition, our instincts, the coded language of the Soul, it means that when the challenges get tough, we can still be kind, understanding, compassionate and forgiving - even when it's hard to do so. It gives us the capacity to stick around. It means consciously focusing on the good side of people, rather than the bad. It means consciously and deliberately making huge efforts to work through our own "negative stuff", for innately our Soul and Spirit longs to improve, to become a better person. And so, our soulmate is someone with whom we can grow. They are not afraid of our independence; in fact, they will encourage it. There will be challenges, but that is okay, it brings to the surface that which needs to be healed. Soulmates are people in our life who can help us to become better people, to reach our full potential, and to grow in Love. So, is Dermot my soulmate? Yes, he is, we are to each other, each of us having the capacity to unlock the potential in the other. But we are also astrologically compatible, the Moon being especially so, ensuring domestic harmony in our daily lives, as we cope with our Twin Flame a mirror image of each other, destined to cause pain, but only through pain can any form of transformation take place. A Twin Flame unearths the dirt on the other enabling cleansing and healing to take place and only when the baggage has been burnt away will their physical connection end.

Of course, not everyone is going to have three husbands, or even two or even one! Each of us has a different Path to follow. But all of us will interface with other people throughout our lifetime. We are biologically designed and programmed to seek companionship or a partner, to fall in love. But only the Soul or the Ego will determine what company we keep. Some people may find their soulmate early in life. Others may never find them. Many people settle for a life partner for a multitude of reasons - perhaps out of routine or habit, perhaps for financial security - but mostly I suspect from a subconscious fear of being alone. Some relationships will be disastrous and detrimental to our well-being: these are learning curves, and part of our mental, emotional, and Spiritual development. Other relationships are urged by the Ego, the Ego within us collaborating with the Ego of others, leading to downfall, exciting greed, flaming lust or cruel violence. The Spirit and Soul will never ask of such things. The Spirit and Soul will turn you away. We have the potential to choose which Path we take. I wish you Love and Blessings in your soulmate search.

Chapter 10

Love, Sex, Lust and Passion

Yet another scandal involving allegations of sexual assault has rocked society. This time in Hollywood, where fiction and non-fiction are blurred in the struggle for fame and fortune. Why should we be surprised? The strength of the sexual urge has the capacity to drive Man to the hidden darkest depths of the Ego, where carnal lust fights for primacy in an omnivorous animal. This time it involves the American film producer, Harvey Weinstein. As more and more women come forward, mostly young aspiring actresses, he is accused of being a serial sexual predator over many years. Like many others before him, such as the British celebrity, Jimmy Savile, Weinstein has used his power, wealth, and celebrity status, not only to force his unwanted intentions onto his victims, but also as a tool to blackmail his victims emotionally and mentally into silence, thus retaining his social and professional status which was a cover-up for further acts of perversion. Of course, this type of perverted sexual behaviour is not just privy to the famous or well-known, it is privy to the common Man as well, and I concede women in that colloquialism. Sexual abuse or harassment does not require a glamorous setting, thriving around the world in multiple, mundane places. In our places of work and worship, in hotels and restaurants, in offices, care homes, hospitals, and places where we expect to feel safe and cared for. It happens in the corridors of power where the ultimate authority resides, such as in Westminster and the White House. It happens in people's homes behind closed doors, the perpetrator often being the least suspected person: a wolf in sheep's clothing ready to pounce on his victim at any time or manipulate his position to gain trust in his targeted victim.

As a young Technical Tracer apprentice working in a drawing office back in the late 1960s, I was often subjected to sexual harassment by members of the male staff who were well into their 40s or 50s. The only way I dealt with it was to say something like, in a very loud voice, "go take a cold shower" or "does your wife and children know you're a sexual predator and bloody nuisance to the female staff at work?" Having caught the attention of everyone around us, the perpetrator would slink away very red-faced! But not to be outdone a rumour would then circulate the office that I was, "a very cold fish with no sense of humour!" Being easy on the eye, as my grandmother used to say, I was often subjected to suggestive, crude remarks, or being touched inappropriately, to downright blatant sexual proposition throughout the 22 years I worked in different drawing offices around Great Britain. The perpetrators were mostly married men with children the same age as me. It has thus never ceased to surprise me how the strength of the sexual appetite can eliminate all sense of social and personal responsibility and morality, feeding into the darkest depths of the Ego, submerging the Spirit so its warnings are ignored.

Sex is innate to all sentient creatures; it is an instinct of nature. But how we use sex as human beings depends entirely on our own personal Spiritual development. As we see above, sex can be used by the Ego for actions of abuse or self-gratification, but it can also be utilised by the Spirit in an expression of Love and greater connection. Spirit is after all an entity of Love, an all-consuming Love. Spiritual Love is not gender orientated; thus, it has no sexual orientations, and is not governed thereof: thus, ruling out the notion of discrimination against lesbians, gays, bisexuals, and transgender people. Spirit is Love, and Love is

Love. Thus, Love born of our Spirit is a caring love for all life on earth, no matter what form the life comes in.

For many people these days, especially the vulnerable young, they have no understanding that sexual intimacy is best expressed within a loving relationship. They might understand the physical biological actions that required intimacy, but they are devoid of any other knowledge that explains this very complex human condition, this biological urge for copulation which is an instinct natural to all sentient life ensuring the species carries on. However, as Man has evolved to the world he now lives in, born of his mental, emotional, psychological, and physical self, he still understands less about what constitutes love, sex, lust and passion and the difference thereof. In keeping with the evolution of Man, the Internet now makes voyeurism "normal" as if peering behind net curtains, enabling the socially "decent" to view pornography in the comfort of their home while allowing the sexually perverted to target and groom young children, innocent victims for adult pornography. And so, for many young people who have grown up with the Internet, their sexual education is often coloured by information found in cyberspace, and for them blurring the boundaries between what is decent loving behaviour and pornography. In fact, we might argue, that in our godless secular societies we are now more ignorant of this innate urge then our predecessors were in times of antiquity.

In times gone by, ancient cultures and societies understood and recognised the many facets to this innate urge, addressing them through mythological deities or gods. Many of us will be familiar with the gods of ancient Greek such as Aphrodite, a goddess of love and sexuality or Eleni, the goddess of sexual pleasure, oral sex, or cunnilingus. Or Hermaphroditus, the god of effeminate men and hermaphrodites, or Hymen, the god of marriage, weddings, and the bridal hymn. The success of a beguiling nature could be found in the god of Pan, a god of sweet talk and flattery, famous for his sexual prowess and his conquest of the Moon goddess, Selene. Pan is often depicted with an erect phallus, warning of his readiness on some poor unsuspecting nymph! Love and lust deities were common in ancient cultures such as the Aztecs and the Chinese and can still be found in modern polytheistic religions such as Hindu. It could also be said that the writers of the Christian Bible recognised the many facets of the sexual urge in the story of Adam and Eve. Warning of the weakness within the human condition, the sexual urge, the Ego that is always tempted by forbidden fruit that can ultimately lead to Man's downfall. Thus, we could say, that ancient cultures and societies not only recognised and made provision for our higher consciousness, our Spirit. But also recognised and made provision for, our lower consciousness, our Ego.

Thus, sex is not just a vehicle that expresses our physical desires, the desires of the flesh, perversions or otherwise, but it is often used consciously or subconsciously to mould or determine our fate and destiny, and with lessons to learn thereof. The two historical figures of Queen Cleopatra and Josephine Bonaparte give a good example of this, but also, if we look closely, they are perhaps examples of more than just physical desire and its utility. The historical interpretation of Cleopatra's life and persona is according to Lucy Hughes Hallett, largely fictitious, concentrating too much on the sexual perversions, diverging away from the real woman and historical events. [20] However, the fact that these erotic fantasies have developed over two thousand years highlights the powerful influence sex has perhaps explaining the popularisation of these two women in theatre, television, and film production. And so, for the purpose of this exercise I draw on the popularised, familiar version of these two women, their personas, and lives which I fully accept are perhaps not historically accurate. Queen Cleopatra of Egypt {69 BC/30 BC} was a mere young teenager when she inherited rule from her father alongside her 10-year-old brother Ptolemy XIII, married him and later went on to marry another young brother, Ptolemy XIV, each with whom she ruled Egypt as husband-and-wife. But these were not harmonious relationships, pitted as they were with political intrigue and murderous rivalry for the throne. No children were born of these relationships, so perhaps they were not consummated, however, the marriage with her brothers, although decreed by tradition, shows us the intensity of Cleopatra's ambitions and allows us to understand the tensions and the underlining factors of sexual promiscuity that underpinned relationships of these times intent on political objectives.

Perhaps it comes as no surprise then that Cleopatra set out to seduce Julius Caesar travelling to the Royal Palace in Alexandria, where she was allegedly carried to Caesar rolled up in a luxurious rug offering herself as a gift at his feet. Inherent to her nature and her upbringing, Cleopatra had learnt the art of sexual allurement. Caesar, a Roman politician, and a brilliant army general, was unable to avoid being captivated by Cleopatra thus agreeing to intercede with the Egyptian civil war, which resulted in defeat for the pharaoh's forces. Caesar went on to install Cleopatra along with her other brother Ptolemy XIV as joint rulers and in celebration of this and their victory in war, a triumphal procession was organised on the River Nile in 47 BC. The Royal barge was accompanied by four hundred additional ships, introducing Caesar to the opulent, hedonistic lifestyle of the Egyptian pharaohs, the aphrodisiacs of power and wealth resulting in intimacy between the two of them, brushing aside other considerations, including that of Caesar's marriage. Caesar continued his adulterous relationship with Cleopatra all through his marriage and is said to have fathered Cleopatra's son whom she named Caesarion, meaning "Little Caesar." But whether Cleopatra had any deep lasting affection for Caesar is debatable. Soon after Caesar's assassination Ptolemy XIV died, thought to have been poisoned by his sister Cleopatra who then made herself and her young son co-rulers. But these were politically charged times, resulting in another Civil War which was temporarily resolved by Octavian, Caesar's great-nephew and chosen heir, and Mark Antony a powerful general and Roman political leader. Mark Antony summoned Cleopatra to answer charges that she had aided his enemies. And once again Cleopatra put into operation a plan to seduce Antony, and she arrived in Tarsus on a magnificent river barge opulently decorated in gold, Cleopatra herself dressed as Venus the god of love. Apparently successful in her efforts, Mark Antony returned Cleopatra to Alexandria where they are said to have spent the winter in debauchery, giving vent to the Ego. Marriage followed (albeit bigamous) and bore three children perhaps to cement their political power. But perhaps also we can assume a growing affection, even love and commitment when we look at how Mark Antony attempted to kill himself upon hearing Cleopatra was dead, and she later is said to have taken her own life from a self-inflicted snakebite. However, before her sad demise it did not stop her from attempting to seduce the triumphant Octavian who resisted her charms. Perhaps for the first time in her life she realised that her sexual prowess no longer served a purpose to further her ambitions. Facing defeat and the prospect of losing her Kingdom to Rome, Queen Cleopatra might have felt that her options were limited. When the Ego rules our lives for self-gratification, whether that is to further ambitions for material gain or career advantage or sexual perversion many of us will come to experience a self-inflicted snakebite metaphorically speaking. A sort of self sabotage, an ending of some sort, a cry for help from our Spirit within. Cleopatra has gone down in history as being assertive and ruthless, using her sexual prowess to advantage her ambitions just like a Venus fly trap lures its victims to death by the pungent smell of its open sticky cactus leaves. Antony and Cleopatra's physical demise was as tragic as their lives, each one using the other to meet their own agendas, failing to find the meaning of True love, a Spiritual Love in their earthly life. [20]

The love affair between Josephine Tascher de la Pagerie {1763/1814} and Napoleon Bonaparte {1769/1821} is another historical story we are all familiar with, often depicting it as the epitome of romance. But maybe we are looking at them through rose tinted glasses, which is what romantic love does to us when caught in its trap, so once again I apologise for any historical inaccuracies. However, my lessons from the Spirit World over the years inform me that Josephine and Bonaparte, like Cleopatra, Caesar, and Mark Antony before them, along with the rest of us who come to earth to live an earthly life, are all born with a life pattern of our times with lessons and challenges thereof which ultimately progress our Spiritual development.

Although ending her life in isolated opulence Josephine did in fact have a rather inauspicious start. At the tender age of 16, she was made to leave her father's struggling sugarcane plantation in Martinique for Paris, where a paternal aunt arranged for Josephine to marry her deceased sister's fiancé, a young aristocrat called Alexandra de Beauharnais. The two were married in December 1779 whereupon a son and daughter followed a few years later. But by all accounts, it was not a happy marriage, her husband thinking her plump and unsophisticated. Her black teeth probably not helping, a throwback to her childhood days where access to sugarcane was detrimental to dental health. Thus, at barely 20 years old, her husband sent Josephine and their children to live in a convent. Josephine made good use of her time there with other abandoned wives, learning the arts of make-up, dress, and behaviour that would befit a true Parisienne. A year later, when her husband decided to reclaim her, Josephine had transformed herself into a beautiful woman. Nevertheless, her husband remained immune to her charms resulting in a court ordered separation. But Josephine's sudden freedom to live as she wished ended as suddenly as it began when during the French reign of Terror, Josephine was widowed when her husband was sent to the guillotine. Josephine, as his wife, was sent to the most brutal prison in Paris, Les Carmes, where women waited in their flimsy linen underdresses, their hair cut short in preparation for the guillotine. But Fate intervened again when on the day before her trial, the government was deposed, and a new one brought in. The executions were immediately halted.

Years before, she had been told by a fortune teller that one day she would be Queen of France - now she was more determined than ever to make it happen. Josephine recovered the possessions of her deceased husband, enabling her to continue the life of high society. Befriending another survivor of prison, the flamboyant socialite Theresa Tallien, Josephine was introduced into the ways of the Parisians who were hungry to celebrate their survival of the Terrors. Eager to embrace life in a come-what-way manner, Josephine and her new friends set out to be daring and outrageous, and with their hair still short, the new fashion was "the prison look." Parties were thrown where the women wore red ribbon around their neck to represent the guillotine, while their dresses were tiny, white, flimsy and revealing. She soon learnt the art of prostituting herself to gain the favours of men in power. It was not long before she became the lover to the wealthy politician and de facto governor of France, Paul Barras. Barras indulged her with a magnificent home and all the trappings thereof, while she indulged him in his debauched desires, playing the charming, sophisticated hostess at his political dinners, while participating in after-dinner entertainment, his orgies. [21]

But a relationship based on the appetite of the Ego soon tires and seeks conquest somewhere else. At the age of thirty, Josephine sensed she needed the security of a husband. At one of Barras's dinners, she was asked to sit next to Napoleon, a sallow faced soldier without money or connections. Josephine saw his potential, and although six years her junior, she soon became Napoleon's mistress, encouraging him to accept a command and improve his status. In just over a year, they married. However, this was not to be wedded bliss. Josephine and Napoleon had affairs, her with a Hussar lieutenant and he with a series of lovers, including her own lady-in-waiting! Regardless of this, the two continued as spouses with Josephine as Napoleon's helpmate, the power behind the throne, masterminding his political career and utilizing her social graces and connections to ensure his influence and prestige grew. With Josephine's support, and astute mind for political manoeuvring, before long Napoleon had ousted Barras thus making himself Consul, before finally Emperor of France. However, Fate intervened once again when due to a lack of producing an heir Josephine came under pressure to divorce Napoleon 14 years later. Napoleon insisted that Josephine retain the title of Empress and that "she ever holds me as her best and dearest friend." Josephine retreated to live in their home near Paris remaining on good terms with Napoleon. She is reputed to have said, "The only thing that ever came between us was my debts, certainly not his manhood."[21]

If these remarks have any truth, does this mean that Josephine is unwittingly informing us that sex was just a means to an end to achieve one's goals? Perhaps his infidelities and his remarriage to gain an heir did not bother her, after all, she had still been the wife to the most powerful man in France, the power behind the throne, having used her newly developed social skills, charms and graces and social position to advance her husband's political fortunes. Can we thus assume that her head ruled her heart while at the same time, like Cleopatra, Josephine would use her sexual charisma to lure in her target? We know she had several affairs before she met Bonaparte, and one soon after they married leading us to assume, she must have been blessed with some level of sexual charisma and was quite capable of using it when needs must! Was it this sexual charisma that drew Bonaparte to her side, therefore he was in lust more than love, at least in the early days? And given that Bonaparte was quite short in stature with little to recommend him in good looks, and often gruff, and aggressive, might we assume he wouldn't have been so lucky with the ladies if he hadn't been the emperor!

In March 1811, Napoleon's new wife delivered him a long-awaited son. Two years later, Napoleon arranged for Josephine to meet the young Prince who had "cost her so many tears." Are we thus to conclude, that despite social and financial considerations, and ensuring the French empire continued, underneath it all, Josephine developed an affection for Napoleon, perhaps love, and that her feelings were reciprocated? On May 29th, 1814, Josephine passed-away having caught a chill a few days earlier while walking in the gardens of their magnificent home Malmaison, just outside Paris. When Napoleon heard the news, he was in exile on Elba. Refusing to see anyone, Napoleon apparently stayed locked in his room for two days. He is reputed to have once told a friend, "I truly loved my Josephine, but I did not respect her." [21] Despite his numerous affairs, eventual divorce and remarriage, Napoleon is said to have called out her name on his dying breath seven years later. Perhaps the strength of the sexual urge, the charisma of some thereof, can turn flames of attraction and arousal into flames that touch the core of our heart.

Of course, we cannot know for certain what motivated Cleopatra and Josephine to take the actions they did, we can only surmise. But still, even though these are historical stories, they are stories of real people, real events as far as historical records show, whose actions born of their emotions we can still relate to today explaining their popularisation in drama. Both women were clever tacticians, using their sexual charisma and sex to survive, to achieve their goals, shaping not only their own destiny in what was essentially, a Man's world, but the destiny of those they interrelated with. We have an idealistic romantic view of love which is why the novelist who writes of it is often successful, highlighting the human urge to transport themselves into a world far removed from the one we live in. The idea of a hero whisking his love off to a faraway place of romance and financial security appeals to the romantic in many of us. Yet romance and real-life are often far removed, which is perhaps why so many of us go through the divorce courts these days. Expectations are high, higher than ever before in previous generations. We now want the best of everything in life, instantly, including in our relationships. And coupled with this attitude, is the lack of determination and perseverance. The lack of self- sacrifice to work things out. The lack of recognising that true love does not come easy, it is not always a free meal! And while we are all looking for that romantic utopia, the gap is filled with egotistical lust, lust of the physical flesh, lust for things we cannot always have in the material world, which is why so many people these days are lost and disillusioned, fuelled by self-inflicted discontentment.

The Ego only seeks self-gratification, for wealth, power, control, and uses sex as a tool of conquest, to control, to intimidate, to abuse and assault. Sex becomes an instrument to determine an outcome, to manipulate, to achieve one's goals, shaping and moulding our fate, our destiny. This side of the human condition is innate to all of us, which is why we can still relate to Cleopatra's and Josephine's story. For some people who choose lust, like the American financier Jeffrey Epstein and his associates, they ultimately discover it is a fleeting passion, leaving the Soul and Spirit crying out for help. Whereas Love born of our Spirit, which is born of our Creator, is fulfilling and lasting and touches all Spirits thereof. For we are all Spirit, our friends, our neighbours, our family, our pets, the natural world, and all Life thereof. And when we choose Love born of our Spirit, all the challenges that impact our life become a lot easier to bear. For life is not perfect, it was never designed to be! Nor was it designed to be abused, sexually or otherwise.

In the context of Spiritual love, the act of sex, "making love" can perhaps be seen as a physical manifestation of an emotional and psychological need. As Spiritual beings we nevertheless exist in physical bodies – and we can express love in all those physical ways – through touch, sight, and sound. For many people, physical acts of love are the most meaningful ways for them to express and understand it – at least between fellow human beings. But Love born of the Spirit does not have to be sexual. It stands alone and can be channelled into anything or anyone thus having a knock-on effect for everything else around it. For true Spiritual Love does not ask for anything back in return. It does not ask you to demoralise yourself. It does not ask you to sacrifice your dreams but encourages you to reach them instead. Spiritual Love will not emotionally, mentally, or physically abuse you. It will not coerce you by applying mental or emotional blackmail. It will not ask you to do anything that makes you feel uncomfortable, sick at heart, or regretful. Spiritual Love will not attempt to undermine your higher consciousness but will encourage you to develop it. It will not lie or deceive you or betray you, it will never let you down. Spiritual Love does not judge you or kick you in the teeth. It is always there for you, no matter what.

Spiritual Love is a caring love, even when life gets tough. Spiritual Love will put others first before the needs of self. Tolerance, consideration, kindness and caring in thought and action is the ultimate expression of Spiritual Love. And when love becomes difficult, compassion is always there. Spiritual Love cannot be broken, it is lasting. There are no boundaries on earth or the universe that can hold it. It lasts and travels through time and space. It goes on beyond our physical demise. For when we open our hearts to Spiritual Love, we are connected for ever-after in this life and beyond.

Chapter 11

Globalisation

As a creature with a love of solitude, I have always hated shopping. I cannot think of anything worse to do with my precious time. When my children were young, I would drop them off at school, dash to the local town and whizz round the supermarket, doing what I had to do as quickly as possible, before rushing back to my home again in the peaceful Somerset countryside. My children are now, as adults, just the same. None of us like shopping and the hustle and bustle of crowded towns and cities that generally comes with it. My husband and I now live on the beautiful west coast of Southern Ireland. Although much has changed over the last 20 years, the small local town of Ennistymon is still typically Irish, serving the local community with traditional small family run businesses, offering all the opportunities for domestic shopping we need. If other commodities are needed such as clothes, shoes, or household items, we travel further afield, usually to Galway or to Ennis and treat it as a day out, having lunch somewhere nice. The shopping part of it then, although it might have been necessary, becomes something pleasant rather than something I should endure.

We still have friends and relatives that live in the UK which we occasionally visit. And each time we do so, it takes a day or two to adjust to the busy, overcrowded hustle and bustle of UK life. It seems to me, that each day of the week is the same, with a lot of people's lives tied up with routine. The routine of daily life, dropping the kids off to school, rushing to work, caught up in gridlock, getting through the day, somehow! Only to repeat the same process at the end of the day or over the weekend.

Everybody seems to be stuck on a perpetual conveyor belt, so caught up in the material world, they cannot find a way to get off. So, they look for an adrenaline kick. A short-term injection of happiness, a foreign holiday if they can afford it, or better still, shopping! Shopping has now become the new religion on a Sunday in the UK. When I was a child, growing up in the late 1940s and 1950s, Sundays were days of respite. They were holy days, which is where the term, holiday comes from. They were days of family worship and opportunities for lingering over a lazy Sunday lunch with loved ones. Sundays were times for family get togethers, to talk, to discuss, to go on long walks, to play games in the park or the garden with one's friends or cousins. Now the idea of family quality time, or personal downtime is to go shopping, either in the high street or on the Internet. Thus, shopping is available to all of us 24/7. And so, Sunday, as with all the other days of the week, has become a day to worship consumerism, feeding into the addiction of spending, acquiring things that for the most part, we don't really need, thus fuelling globalisation. The UK is not alone in this of course. The new religion of consumerism has now engulfed the Western world, tormenting the Third World, exploiting other countries for their cheap labour, even child labour sometimes, while their environments are ravaged. Despite employment, their low wages and substandard employment conditions often mean they remain on the fringes of their society, while playing a vital role in producing the goods that fuels the West's addiction.

Unwittingly, and unintentionally the West's addiction for consumerism usually means huge benefits for the few. While those in poverty coexist, leaving them marginalised, often poorly educated, or suffering from ill-health, excluded from globalised induced opportunities, increasing ethnic tensions, social and civil unrest, revolution, even war. The notion of consumerism and the material wealth thereof has become a goal that the world population is reaching for. No matter where we live, what country we live in or our social level, the notion that one is wealthy enough to participate in consumerism now equates to personal happiness for many people. Thus, the West's addiction for consumerism, like a cancer, is spreading. On the one hand, creating a rapid deterioration of the natural environment, the potential to spread new diseases through international trading and travel, while at the same time, increasing poverty and alienation. Whereas those in the West continue to seek that elusive elixir of life, that special "something" that can fill the empty void "within" that so many people these days suffer from. That inner emptiness that is now being filled with a kick of adrenaline that comes with another purchase, or another foreign holiday! Many people in the West would claim they are hard up, but are they? They still manage to find the money to feed their addiction to consumerism.

On the 8th of August 2017, the Irish television network RTE presented a documentary about Ireland not belonging to the Irish anymore. It was a documentary about "vulture" funds, so-called because of the way they wait and feed off the dying and the vulnerable. [22] Vulture funds are facilitated by faceless, unregulated, corporate investors. People that have accumulated massive wealth and power who have the capacity to purchase national debt worldwide, taking ownership of national banks, mortgage lenders, and large and small family businesses that have accumulated financial debt. These people and their vulture funds operate under clandestine conditions, surreptitiously inveigling their way into countries, undermining, and strangling their economies, political policies, and sovereignty on the pretext of helping them out of a sticky financial crisis, when in truth they are there to make huge financial gain on the back of other people's misery. Misfortune born of personal and/or government overspending is consumerism at its worst. These people destroy lives with strangling interest rates and their ruthless, heartless repossession policies, ruining people's livelihoods, taking away their homes. This is globalisation at its worst, extortion at the highest level, perpetrated by the Ego raining supreme accumulating more wealth for the wealthy few, while weakening and eroding freedom for the masses. We continue to live with the fallout of the banking crisis of more than 10 years ago. Ireland is not alone in this; the fallout went viral. The worldwide disease of consumerism born of the Ego means we only have ourselves to blame! We might prefer to blame other people, the government, politicians, the banks, agents beyond our control. But at the end of the day, the buck stops with us. Each of us is responsible for own spending habits, ensuring we spend within our means, living in accordance with our Spirit as opposed to our Ego. Our spending and borrowing has a rippling effect on the wider world.

Of course, we could argue, that consumerism, thus globalisation has been with us since the beginning of time. It is part of Man's evolution. Globalisation is nothing new. Indeed, we might say, that the religions of Christianity, Islam and Buddhism globalised on the back of migration, imperialists, evangelists, missionaries, and traders. Beginning as a barter, its inherent within Man to trade with his neighbour. Exchanging commodities, knowledge, and information, absorbing what we want to absorb, discarding others, colouring, and flavouring indigenous traditions and cultures. Early civilisations such as the Sumer and the Indus Valley of the third millennium BCE, ancient Greece, the old-world centres of China, Japan, Indian, Persia, Europe and Arabia were all built on trade links, some of them opening-up long-distance political and economic interactions between their civilisations. Later, around the 1600s, Western states adapted and implemented traditional ideas from the East, travelling by horse, camel or foot across Asia, North Africa, the Middle East, and certain parts of Europe. There was no interference with independent states or countries. This early form of globalisation was simply interested in trade and cultural exchange. But by the late 19th century, globalisation was characterised by the rise of maritime European empires of the 16th and 17th centuries, opening-up international trade links with imperialist countries. In modern parlance, we could say, that globalisation began with the invention of steam mechanism, the advent of the Industrial Revolution in the 1820s, developments in transport systems, developing further as we progressed into the 20th century when the world's economies and cultures grew very quickly. Industrialisation standardised household items which in turn encouraged rapid growth in both population and demand for its commodities. [23] Thus, consumerism was born, feeding into the development of globalisation as we know it today. Developing discontent within those that have, and those that have not. Submerging the Spirit, giving vent to the Ego.

As communications continue to open-up and develop there are highs and lows to it all. Not long ago, mobile phones looked like large boxes used only by the army on manoeuvres. But by the late 1980s, although still large and clumsy by today's standards, mobile phones had become small enough to be held by hand and available for public use. Very quickly our "connectedness" has developed and increased. Since the 1990s, communication has really opened-up via our computers and the Internet. Many of us now work from home and/or socialise, interrelating, interfacing, reaching a worldwide audience without regard to our geographical personal location. The invention of personal computers, the Internet, our smart phones, social network sites has connected us on a level never known before. Increasingly, we see Spirit at work using the Internet to influence public policies, attitudes, and opinions across national boundaries for the benefit of charities, philanthropic organisations, environmental and animal welfare institutions. We now share similar interests in sport, music, fashion, and technology. The modern Olympic Games has athletes from more than two hundred nations, while the FIFA World Cup is apparently the most widely viewed and followed sporting event in the world, exceeding that of the Olympic Games; where a ninth of the entire world population watched the 2006 World Cup final, these events highlighting the connectedness of similar taste. In many ways we are different, but the same! We also see the Ego using the Internet to access and promote negativity, sometimes dark forces that are detrimental to the Soul. As with anything else in this Life, knowledge or technology can advance our civilization and society but it depends on whether we have applied our Ego or Spirit.

Developments in technology, aviation and transport infrastructure have enabled this "connectedness" to take place. Since the Second World War we have seen the invention of the shipping container which have advanced globalisation of commerce, along with politicians from major governments who have laid down frameworks for international monetary policies, founding institutions to facilitate economic growth by lowering trade barriers. I remember in the early 1960s, friends of my parents went to Paris for a week. It was the talk of the neighbourhood for the rest of the year. Only the rich and famous or well-heeled could afford foreign holidays in those days. Now every man, woman and child and their dog seem to vacate abroad, it being more common rather than the exception. Over the last three or four decades, we have seen massive increase in cheap package holidays enabling millions of people throughout the year to travel to other parts of the world, opening-up communications and enjoying the experience of foreign cultures, people, and traditions. At the same time, with cheaper aviation came "open sky" policies and low-cost carriers which has helped to bring commercial competition to the market, enabling all of us to enjoy food from foreign countries at affordable prices throughout the year. Agreements between countries, such as the Schengen agreement has allowed citizens of other countries to travel between them without a visa. The European Union for example, means that people can move freely between member states to live, work, study or retire in a country other than their birth country. At the same time, there has been a rapid growth of students who seek higher education in a foreign country, many of whom use their studies as a steppingstone to apply for citizenship. And so, as we globalise ourselves through international travel, is it any surprise that we globalized diseases? Emerging "superbugs" with resistance to antibiotics have been tracked spreading across the globe over the last few decades, and mosquito-borne infections from Africa and South America have become established in the United States. Many years ago, I was informed by Spirit that a pandemic was coming down the road. So frightened was I of this prediction that I phoned my son in the United States. Working as a professor of paediatrics and being a director of infectious diseases, I felt he might have some information on this topic. Nicholas, as my eldest child has always been aware of my Spiritual connections, so was not at all surprised at what I told him. The Spirit world he said, are only telling me what scientists have known for some time! That indeed a pandemic is forecast, it is just a question of when! Now in the mist of Covid 19 my Spiritual informers tell me there is worse to come if we do not mend our ways! Is it perhaps Mother Nature sending us a message, warning us of our global excesses? Certainly, many of us have become acutely aware of our impact on the world, and our need for connectedness to our Spiritual essence during this time.

In as much as consumerism is linked into globalisation, it affects us for better or worse, in accordance with whether we are influenced by our Spirit or the Ego. Each of us can impact the world and its environment and all species thereof in accordance with our behaviour and our actions. Now we can globalise our thoughts, our words, our actions, our shopping habits, our diseases which in turn have a rippling effect on the wider community. If we take time to think about our attitudes, opinions, actions, and spending habits, what we are purchasing, what is it made of, where has it come from: 'Do I really need it?", "Do I really need to go away on that foreign holiday?" - then perhaps we can begin to address some of the world's problems. We can begin to address the mountains of waste that come with consumerism. The throwaway mindset. We can begin to address the pollution of our air, sea, and soil. We can begin to address climate change. We can begin to address exploitation, poverty, and inequality. We can begin to address our attitude towards the natural world and all other species thereof. For we are part of the natural world, we are not separate from it because all life on planet Earth takes its form from the same beginning, a Universal Creative Force, an energy, a Super Consciousness, a Spiritual essence, that ripples through, connecting and linking all Life thereafter no matter what form it takes. And here lies the crux of the matter. Scientists now tell us that the problems that are currently impacting planet Earth are a direct result of human activity. But as a child tutored by Spirit, I have long known you cannot abuse, pillage and exploit nature and all other life forms thereof without it being detrimental to the Soul of Life, the Soul of planet Earth, a life support system which includes the human species. In other words, because Homo sapiens are as much part of the natural world as all other species, it follows that if you abuse, pillage, and exploit the natural world, the Homo sapiens too will suffer. And now we see Mother Nature fighting back, informing us through Her coded language all is not well, hence we suffer climate crisis, fire, and flood, - collapse of biodiversity and ecosystems, mass extinction, global pollution, and pandemics. If we continue to live by Ego incentive consumerism, there is worse to come!

And so, globalisation begins in our mindset, our actions and words, our homes, it is local, it is regional, it is national, it is international. It incorporates social and economic relations and networks which are organised on a local and national basis. These in turn can develop into regional and global interactions underpinning a transformation in the organisation of human affairs, for better or worse, linking us all together and expanding human activity across regions and continents. Globalisation brings about the process of world shrinkage, enhancing communication from one side of the world to the other, with mutual benefits for all concerned, or it can do the opposite. It involves the circulation and exchange and transmission of different institutions, organisations, and policies as well as the movement of commodities and other objects of exchange. It involves the transmission of ideas, diseases, notions and images, knowledge, and information. It involves the institutions and policies of worldwide banking along with financial investments which can impact us all for better or worse!

As we proceed on our journey of evolution, a journey involving the Spirit and Ego how we go forward in this process depends which faculty in Man wins! Currently the Ego is the driving force of our modern world and all things thereof which is not sustainable and will only lead to Man's downfall. But there is hope, we can do our Best to turn the tables. I have been informed by Spirit and the Angels that if we can apply our Spiritual attributes, we can become more Spiritually attuned, more able to be inclusive, more able to embrace our differences. Thus, globalisation will take on a new meaning, the concept of a world citizen, the notion that as a human being we all have a responsibility towards each other. At the same time, as a world citizen, we will come to understand the responsibility we have towards the environment, the natural world and all other species that reside within it. In this increasingly globalised world, world citizens will develop over time their higher consciousness, thus their mindset of this shared responsibility. Globalisation is inevitable, it is part of human evolution. It is what we have been doing since the beginning of time. But currently, we are going through a period of conflict between the Ego and the Spirit and all the highs and lows this process brings. What side of our personas comes out on top depends on us. We can develop respect for Life, for each other and for other lifeforms, no matter what form the life takes. We can learn to live in harmony with the natural world and all species thereof. We can learn to live in harmony with each other despite differences in religion, gender, race, cultural traditions, ethnicity, and/or social positions.

We are already beginning to see changes in attitudes and opinions as both the UK and Southern Ireland have embraced, through political policies equality for same-sex couples, enabling them to get married, having access to the same legal rights as heterosexual couples, acknowledging and celebrating that Love is Love. This is a sign of the emergence of humanity's higher consciousness, our Soul mindset shown by the masses in displays of emotionally and defiant opposition against violence after another murder, or terrorist attack, or after a military invasion on a sovereign country. Over time, the same mindset and principles will involve many other aspects to our lives across the globe. Instead of focusing on our differences, which in the end, we can learn are few, we can become more integrated and more aware of common interests and a sense of shared humanity which will enrich our lives. We are at the beginning of a very long period where if we choose to live according to our Spirit we can learn to live under a shared umbrella, while at the same time, retaining our indigenous traditions, our own belief systems and ethnic and/or gender individuality. We may then be able to say, as

Plutarch is quoted as saying to Socrates, “I am not an Athenian or a Greek, but a citizen of the world.”

Chapter 12

Food for Thought

Mention the word Spirit, and you will get one of two reactions: either people will associate Spirit with religion, or they imagine it to be a ghostly apparition floating about as depicted on some Hollywood set. But the truth is, Spirit is neither of these things. It is phenomena, innate in all of us on planet Earth, whether animate or inanimate. It is the vital, immaterial force, the core of all existence and energy emanated out into the universe itself, the philosophy of animatism. Pythagoras {c. 580/500 BC.} and Plato {c.428/347BC} first advanced this hypothesis, which as a Spiritual Medium, I entirely agree with. And like Pythagoras, I believe we can understand and connect with this vital, immaterial force through genres such as music, creativity, geometry, and arithmetic. They help our insights and understanding into the universe. They give access to another dimension, a dimension that is entirely guided and overseen by Spirit and/or the Angels, and it is this other dimension, this "other world" this "other reality" that we all pass onto and that the Spiritual Medium can link into. Thus, when we think of Spirit, it is the energy that emanates all life, no matter what form the life comes in and collectively Spiritual energy emanates from Mother Nature.

When all is well with individual creatures, the Spirit glows, there is balance within, there is health and well-being. Instinct or intuition is the coded language of Spirit for all Life. In sentient beings, it hits the solar plexus, which is the inbuilt GPS that enable the correct choices to be made. Spirit is the guiding force, it works *for* Life, not against it. Ego does the opposite. When you work against nature, that weakens or destroys this coded language, there is imbalance, there is chaos, there is suffering, decay and death. Like stroking a cat's back against the fabric of the fur, the cat becomes agitated and will eventually bite you back!

This is what Mother Nature does when you abuse her and all her family. Nature is a protective Mother. She may stand back as we evolve to greater achievements, but if we go too far, at the expense of other life on this planet, she will hit back to remind us of she's still there! She will remind us of her strict rules concerning practices and behaviour. She will remind us of her strict code of conduct. She will remind us to work within the pattern of night and day, to work with the seasons, to understand the meaning of "going with the flow." She will remind us that all life on planet Earth is there for a reason, and if one link goes missing, or is damaged, then the cycle of Life is weakened. She will remind us, that while she is a caring parent, if we break the rules, there are always consequences, to our selfish, careless actions, and she will have no choice but to administer punishment. Planet Earth, and all life thereof is self-regulating, which is what climate change is all about! It adjusts to meet the circumstances.

As farmers, my maternal grandparents lived and worked within daylight hours, with the seasons, with the flow of nature. They had profound respect and empathy for the natural world and all life thereof. They took nothing for granted and wasted nothing. I have inherited their instincts and ethos, along with inherited Spiritual Mediumship from my paternal great aunts, Grace, and Mary. These inherent attributes have enabled me, all through my life, to not only be able to "read" the energy of the natural world, but also all sentient creatures, no matter what their size. Thus, it comes as no surprise that I have always had a great love of the countryside, the animal kingdom, and an empathy for its joy, and at times its suffering. It is also no surprise, that when it comes to eating meat, it conflicts with my love of animals. Thus, I have always struggled with my conscience, with what I know intuitively, what Spirit has taught me, and with what I have been conditioned to accept by society and my upbringing. But over my lifetime, through my own life experiences of animal husbandry and Spiritual healing, I have come to realise and understand that other animals have feelings too, just like you and me. They can feel pain, joy, fear, and distress. They can feel thirst and hunger. They can feel temperature fluctuation. They can feel anxiety and loneliness when separated from their own kind. Every species has its own language, communicating to its own kind within its own environment. Consequently, all species on planet Earth will have their own worldview. But other animals have something else, that Homo sapiens have dismissed at their peril. And that is, other animals are still in touch with their innate link to Mother Earth. Or at least they would be, given half a chance, if they and their environments were not being destroyed by the Ego of Man. Even our domesticated animals still have innate inherited links to their wild past.

As a child, my grandparent's farm was like heaven on earth. It was a mixed farm, farmed organically, although grandad would not have called it that, it was just the way he'd always done things. In the heart of Dorset, grandad grew crops of wheat and barley, and kale and mangles to feed his cows, rotating the crops regularly and leaving at least one field to go fallow every year, ensuring the land was rested and given over to wildlife. He made silage from the lush organic grass, and hay from his meadows, capturing the scented aroma of mid-summer flora, parcelled up until unwrapped for the cow's nostrils, stimulating their taste buds. Like a dog's nose, the muzzle of the cow conveys all sorts of information to them from their environment, right down to detecting fear within another cow from their urine. Like their ancestors before them, the cow is a grazing animal and loves the scent of fresh grass and clover. Like being told to play in the fields, cows that have been overwintered in barns can still be seen running out of their winter shelter like children, such is their excitement. The smell of fresh grass and the countryside can lift all of us, it does for me. As does silage mixed with molasses and the warm scent of fresh hay, which takes me right back to my childhood on the farm of more than 60 years ago. In those days, grandad's cows were like an extension to the family. Yes, grandad was a farmer, practical in many ways and not given over to sentimentality. But he also recognised that his cows were sentient creatures, with minds of their own, with characteristics, personalities, and feelings. He was a hands-on farmer who recognised their individual traits, how one might be stubborn, how one might have a habit of kicking out, how one always wanted to be first, how one was always last. He believed, the more you handled your farm animals, the better the relationship. And so, he recognised, that cows are warm blooded, tactile creatures, gentle and placid. They are peace loving creatures which is perhaps why the Hindus regard the Cow as Sacred.

Years later, I was to apply the same hands-on approach with my goats, connecting with them, helping to understand their personalities and traits, enabling a bond of trust and affection to develop between us. Critics might argue that a bond between humans and domesticated animals is just a fanciful notion -that we are somehow simply transplanting our humanistic sentimentalities on to another creature - but scientific research done by the Queen Mary University in London showed that goats are very intelligent and quite capable of forming bonds with human beings through complex communication, in much the same way as our pet dogs, cats and horses do. The researchers of this study hoped that their findings would lead to a better understanding of livestock thus an improvement in animal welfare in general. [24] Perhaps we could argue that this research simply underscores what my grandfather, myself and many others like us already knew from instinct, experience and a hands-on approach! Isn't it thus likely that other sentient animals are quite capable of responding to kindness, consideration and TLC and will reciprocate accordingly in their own way? A study done by a Japanese scientist, Miho Nagasawa, and his colleagues, found that levels of oxytocin, the "cuddle hormone", increased in human subjects when their pet dogs were exposed to a dose of the same. [25/26] Oxytocin is an important hormone which measures love in mammals. In humans our brain produces the hormone, which is released when we care about someone, a lover, a friend, a child, a pet. It is the bondage hormone produced by a mother on the birth of her child. Thus, this study provided evidence that when a warm tactile connection is made, a human/animal bond can exist. Surely this research teaches us, that other sentient creatures are quite capable of forming bonds, thus showing us that they, not only have a level of joined up thinking, i.e., intelligence, but feelings too?

I never knew that cows could be aggressive until recent times, when I have heard stories of people being chased or attacked by a cow causing serious injury or resulting in fatality. Perhaps these stories underline the fact, which farming these days distances itself from a hands-on approach of a sentient creature. My grandfather taught me that cows have good memories and will respond accordingly to previous experiences of handling. With their mammalian brain, they never forget a previous experience, or a familiar face! They have ears that move independently of each other, allowing them to pick up sounds from more than one direction at a time. And their large eyes on the side of their faces, enable them to see all around them, thus helping them to determine danger and to remember where the danger came from. Perhaps aggression in cows is a response to suspicion or fear of humans! Grandad used to tell me, "Cows are not stupid, never underestimate them." "They have their own language; they communicate to each other." "And they know what they like, and what they don't like!" Grandad's hands-on approach helped him understand the animals in his keep. He knew intuitively that his cows had a level of joined-up thinking, in that they could distinguish between sweet, salty, bitter and sour food. And that they would avoid eating anything toxic, preferring instead sweet, high calorific foods, the salt lick or the lush pasture of a clover meadow that maintain optimal ruminal good health. Many of us would have seen herds of cows in a filthy state, covered in excrement from their muddy, filthy environment. Yet in a natural environment, in a field where they can spread out, they will avoid eating grass in areas contaminated by faeces of other cows, nor apparently will they graze in areas contaminated by sheep, highlighting an innate hygiene instinct.

In factory farming, cows are kept in large open-ended barns, lying on concrete scattered with minimal straw or hay in a crowded environment, sometimes in their hundreds, sometimes in their thousands, surrounded by excrement which is cleaned away by machines. They are fed on concentrates, silage, and hay devoid of any meadow goodness, and often supplemented with antibiotics to prevent infections from their high-calorie diet. There is no hands-on approach here, only farmworkers that come and go. But my grandad, over many years was able to "read" the energy of those in his care, and he built up a warm relationship with "his girls" based on mutual trust, personalising them with names like, Blossom, Primrose, Bluebell and Buttercup or Gertrude. He took the same approach with everything on the farm thus making it almost self-sufficient. His motto always was, "You've got to work with nature, you've got to read the signs."

Besides its acreage of lush green fields, edged neatly with traditionally laid hedges, bushes and trees, there was a large orchard of pear, apple and plum trees. And a little further on, the large pond fed by a natural spring, where the watercress grew, fighting for survival with the tadpoles in the spring, and a multitude of dragonflies, water boatmen, and other creatures that relied on this watery home.

A little distance from the house, behind a massive red brick wall, lay grandad's very large Victorian vegetable garden where every conceivable seasonal vegetable and herb were grown, including soft fruit in the summer. Flowers were grown amongst the edible foliage, not just for the house, but more importantly, to keep pests at bay. Grandad used to spend many hours in his garden, despite the intensive manual labour of the farm. He once told me, that turning the sod lifted his Spirit, it made him feel good about life. "There's nothing like seeing things grow, to give you a sense of well-being" he would say in his gruff West Country dialect. Grandad knew what he was talking about. Recent scientific research has discovered that when gardening and turning over the soil, a certain micro bacterium acts like antidepressants, is released into the air, stimulating serotonin production within us, thus producing a sense of well-being. {BBC "Countryfile Autumn Diaries" [27] Is this why so many gardeners are happy people and why many other people long to reconnect with Mother Earth? If we have this instinct to connect with the soil because it gives us a sense of well-being, surely it must be so for other sentient creatures we keep locked up under appalling confined conditions in factory farming? My grandparents were very practical, no-nonsense people. They certainly would not have considered themselves emotional or sentimental. When it came to make hard business decisions about the farm and all the animals thereof, they could, if they had to. But their ethos and approach to the animals on the farm, while in their care, was one of respect, consideration, understanding, that they and all Life were connected to the great outdoors. Factory farming animals on the scale it is today would be abhorrent and alien to them.

Besides grandad's beautiful dairy cows, which were always friendly and approachable, along with their husband, Billy the bull (who could be cantankerous at times), a selection of hens and ducks were kept on the farm wandering freely in the orchard and surrounding fields, along with a couple of geese that were fattened up for Christmas. Down by the woods, Granny also kept a couple of beehives which were overseen by her son, uncle Sunny, where honey was collected for the house. The making of this golden nectar would start in the spring when the bees woke up to an array of spring flowers. You could find bees buzzing all over the farm, including other insect life and butterflies, taking in nectar from primroses, bluebells, woodland anemones, buttercups and celandines and the beautiful blossoms in the orchard, before the abundant flora of the vegetable garden or the Meadows burst into bloom. It was here one day, as a child, I was informed by my Spiritual Guide, my great grandmother, Mary Anne Cheek, that bees turn the wheels of all life. And without bees, there is no life on planet Earth. These words now sit heavy in my heart, as environmentalists and conservationists now warn us, our greatest pollinators are now at risk, and it is all down to Man's behaviour. [28 {p.60/70}]

At one time, grandad also kept a few pigs who would wander a small field churning up the soil. Domestic pigs have evolved over thousands of years from wild hogs through human use and intervention. From being a fast, aggressive, tough animal that was difficult to hunt, the domestic pig is now a slow animal, bred for convenience and its meat. Pigs are omnivorous animals, and if farmed organically, still retain their ancestors love of rooting around in the woods, or an orchard, or a field, chomping through fallen apples, grain, acorns, roots, slugs, or worms. My grandparents always said, the meat on a pig who had eaten apples was always much sweeter and tastier. Later, grandad sold his pigs to a neighbouring farmer who bred them on a larger scale, but they still wandered freely in a huge field. Sometimes I would wander over to the neighbour's farm and just stand and watch these grubby animals. They always appeared to be happy to be filthy. I used to wonder why they loved wallowing in the mud, yet they also loved it when their house was cleaned out and laid with new straw. Piglets particularly loved the smell of fresh straw, it seemed to excite their senses, stimulating a game of "catch me if you can." A sow is an attentive mother, overseeing her babies' safety wherever they go, or lying on her side on clean, soft straw, communicating with soft grunts of contentment as her babies suckle. But after her babies are weaned both mother and offspring will try to outwit each other for food, or to be first to a clean bed. So, despite the general appearance of sloth attitude and behaviour, they are quite fast when it comes to self-preservation. Their instincts are competitive, they love to come first. But even so, while preserving this level of independence they are still gregarious and sociable animals, communicating with their own language of grunts and snuffling as they go about their own business, always ensuring they are in touch with each other.

Forcing them to live in an artificial environment of factory farming, where they are densely packed together, separated from a world that stimulates their senses, to a world of concrete, artificial light and contaminated air is therefore cruel and barbaric. The pig has now become a breeding machine. Although now illegal in the EU, many countries still incarcerate a pregnant sow in a despicable manner within a deplorable gestation crate, restricting her movements completely. Mr Dyer, the neighbouring farmer once told me in his broad Dorset dialect, "Never judge a porky by the way it looks." "They're very intelligent creatures with minds of their own." "They may be slow like me but they know what's good for 'em!" I learnt many years later, that pigs do not have sweat glands, so wallowing in mud is a cooling mechanism. They have limited tolerance to elevated temperatures thus can be prone to heat stress which can lead to death if not addressed soon enough. So, wallowing in mud has nothing to do with an enjoyment of getting dirty in the way that humans might see it. It is an action that gives the pig a sense of well-being. It is an act of pure instinct, an act of survival which does not cancel out their enjoyment of a clean bed made of fresh straw. In factory farming, the temperature of their enclosed prison is ventilated and monitored. If it gets too warm, automation kicks in to adjust the problem and the pigs are cooled via a drip water system as they lay on their concrete floor. Thus, there is nothing natural about their factory environment. And just because their physical and instinctive requirements are addressed, at a very basic level, it does not cancel out the fact that there is nothing natural about it. The pig is still devoid of the rich smell of the soil, of grubbing about to find his food, of expressing his instincts to wallow in the mud, of breathing in fresh air. As a child, I used to wonder about the hypocrisy of Mr Dyer who bred pigs for other people to eat, but once told me, "I could never eat a pig, they are far too intelligent." "It would be like, eating a friend!" Research done by Lori Marino, a neuroscientist and founder of the Kimmela Centre for Animal Advocacy, and Christina M Colvin, a professor at Emory University, USA found that pigs are mentally and emotionally complex, sharing many traits with animals we consider intelligent such as dogs and chimpanzees. [29]

Back in the 1940s and 1950s, farming was on the brink of embracing a new world of chemicals, fertilisers, and intensification. Grandad held out for a while, the nearest he got to "modernisation" was to purchase a couple of tractors to replace his old shires which he retired off as old age descended upon them. His old working horses had gone by the time I was around. But Grandad was of the old school, despite the ascending new world, the animals he worked with, were his friends, not just beasts of mere commodity. He had built up a relationship with them over many years, built on trust from both parties, suffering with them when their pregnancies went wrong, or some other health condition had befallen them, and getting excited in their joy of the birth of a healthy calf - adding to his stock of domesticated bovine friends. Often grandad could be found having deep and meaningful conversations with "his girls" while they were being milked (a habit he had got into from his hand milking days), or with Billy the bull, while feeding him or cleaning out his stall. Even later, when the milking parlour was extended and modernised to make room for his growing herd, the considerate attachment for all his bovine friends continued to exist right up until my grandparent's farm was sold on their retirement in the 1960s.

From these early experiences, and the messages I received from Spirit as a child, I learnt a lot about farm animals and came to realise that they too have feelings, and are conscious of themselves, in that there is self-preservation, thus they have their own worldview. For example, chickens are gregarious creatures, and will establish a (literal!) pecking order within the flock, with dominant individuals coming out on top. And woe betide anyone who thinks otherwise - protesters will literally get it in the neck as squabbling ensues. This could also happen when young or new hens are introduced to an existing flock, but usually these disruptions are temporary. Mostly, chickens are communal creatures, sharing food, even sharing nesting boxes or favourite places to lay their eggs, living peacefully once their social order has been established. The rooster is kingpin, usually overseeing his flock from a height or respectable distance. He usually will not get involved with the squabbling of his girls, preferring to take a superior approach as befitting a rooster who not only has responsibilities to maintain the flock, but also to oversee the safety of them. He can be a protective husband and dad, calling to his girls and children to eat first when there is food about. Or crowing loudly, sending out territorial messages in a high-pitched cluck to those that seek to undermine him, or when there is a predator afoot. Both mother hens and roosters will call their chicks to eat. Communication with baby chicks begins just before hatching, the mother hen will hear her babies making gentle peeping noises inside the eggs. She will gently cluck back, stimulating and encouraging her unborn chicks to break out their shells. But sadly, these natural instincts are not privy to what takes place in the artificial world of factory farming where thousands of eggs are incubated in machines providing a computer-controlled environment. This means the chick hatches under false conditions, with only the company of other chicks beside it, crowding its artificial environment with bundles of yellow fluff, instinctively chirping out a distressed call for a mother it did not meet. Naturally, a mother hen will be fiercely protective of her clutch for several weeks, brooding over them to keep them warm, leading them to food and water, clucking out a quiet language, guiding them towards some juicy morsel. Dad is also there to do his share. But a chick on a factory farm will be deprived, not only of this natural relationship with its parents, its guiding force, but also deprived for the rest of its life of the sun on its back, fresh air, and scratching in the soil to find grubs to eat and/or, a dust bath to make. Cleanliness is next to godliness in a chicken's world.

The ancestors to the chicken are the Asian red junglefowl so it is hardly surprising they will wander far and wide, to scratch and forage the ground. When my husband and I lived in the Northumberland countryside, with 10 acres as our back garden, every morning, when let out of the safety of their large cosy wooden henhouse, our Black Rock hens, which we had rescued, would disappear over the brow of the hill into a bordering copse, only to return hours later, their bellies full, with grubs, worms, insects, seeds or fruits, nature's harvest, as befitting an omnivorous creature. Another favourite place was a dry, dusty, loose patch of soil just inside the open barn where they were always guaranteed a dust bath. First one, then two, then maybe three or four would gather at a time, feathers flying, wings outstretched vying for room, shoving out its neighbour in an effort for more dust. This was communal, dry bathing at its best, an important activity for any self-respecting hen to keep on top of parasites that may invade her body and/or feathers.

The story of their rescue is one that illustrates what good care can achieve in an animal's wellbeing. Being keen to establish a small flock of rescued hens, we answered an advert selling Black Rock chickens. When we arrived, the owner explained that she was getting rid of them "because they weren't laying". One look told me why – their indoor environment, although not caged, was filthy and crowded, the air contaminated with the stifled heavy smell of ammonia, a disgusting sign of rotting chicken excrement. With no access to the outside world, clearly the floor of this small barn had not been cleaned out for years, resulting in the spread of diseases, leaving the chickens looking sickly, bedraggled, and skinny, their feathers dull, and in many cases falling out. The idea of this so-called, "free range" housing was a joke and clearly the inhabitants were suffering as a result, so we very quickly agreed to take not only the dozen that we had agreed on, but as many as we could physically put in the car!

The chickens were in such poor health that a few sadly did not even make it back to our home, but the survivors were given free rein over our 10-acres, as well as a secure henhouse and a large barn for shelter, and plenty of warm and dry straw. We fed them grain and mash, and left-over vegetables and other food that we mashed up from our own dinners. The change was astonishing - within weeks of their rescue from their battery imprisonment, our flock of a dozen hens turned from scrawny wrecks, into beautiful, healthy birds, laying large, golden yolk eggs in appreciation. The rich flavour of an egg from a free-range happy hen cannot be compared to what you can buy in the supermarket.

A hen's natural instincts is to lay eggs in a nest which it makes on the ground. Some of our hens did just that having found some old straw on the floor of the barn. But mostly, they took advantage of their wooden straw-lined cosy nest boxes, slightly elevated off the ground which they reached by a couple of perches within their large henhouse. A happy healthy hen might lay one or two eggs a day. But if the hen goes broody, an instinct to just sit, then it will rarely leave its nest until a clutch is complete, anything between eight and twelve eggs. At this point, the hen will stop laying more eggs and just focus on incubating the eggs already laid. If a rooster has done his job, only fertilised eggs will develop into chicks after an incubation period of 21 days. During this time, the hen might lose a few feathers, and become quite defensive if you try to move her, rarely leaving the nest to eat, drink or take a dust bath. To encourage broodiness in a hen, I used to place a couple of china eggs in the nest box, something my grandmother taught me to do when I was a child. To discourage broodiness, the hen is encouraged to use an elevated nesting box with a wire floor. This practice is normally only needed short-term, until the hen gets over her broodiness which does not take long. She soon discovers that the wire floor is most uncomfortable, discouraging any nesting instincts she might have, but factory farming has taken this practice to the cruellest extremes.

Modern egg laying breeds rarely go broody these days because chickens are kept in wire cages for the duration of their short laying life. There was some improvement in Britain when an EU ban on battery cages came into effect on 1st January 2012. [30] At this stage, within the UK, an "enriched cage" was introduced to replace the previous single prison the hen was forced to exist in. Now chickens can exist together in larger prisons, anything between 10 and 86 inmates, all coexisting within their "enriched" environment that provides nest areas, a littered scratching area, perches, and a claw shortening device. Sounds great doesn't it, until you work it out, that the new 750 cm^2 allocated for each inmate within this "colony system" isn't much bigger than the previous amount of space the hen had in solitary confinement. The system of battery hens still exists no matter how you try to dress it up. Conditions are still horrendous for millions of chickens around the world, even within the EU, as thirteen nations have still not complied to the new law. Thus, millions of chickens continue to suffer in silence, existing in uncomfortable, undersized wire cages, stacked on top of each other, with barely enough room to turn around, unable to stretch their wings, unable to stand correctly, unable to behave like a sentient creature. In some countries, like the United States, chickens are not protected in law. Many live out their life, in an artificial environment under artificial lighting day and night, trapped, just eating, drinking and defaecating, cramped with other chickens existing under appalling conditions as laying machines.

Sometimes, false moulting is used rather than slaughter, to reinvigorate egg laying in a chicken. Moulting is natural to all birds, when their old plumage is replaced with new feathers during which time, they may reduce their feed intake, lose a little bodyweight, and suspend reproduction. But taken to extremes, in the artificial environment of factory farming, this practice is considered cruel in the UK and Europe and is thus illegal. It involves the complete withdrawal of food and sometimes water, until the chicken has sufficiently lost enough weight, between seven and fourteen days, to cause the feathers to fall out, thus invigorating egg production. According to the World's Poultry Science Journal, more than 75% of all flocks in the USA underwent false moulting in 2003, prolonging their agony as egg laying machines. [31] Other chickens bred for their flesh are known as broilers and are kept in large houses, thousands at a time, free to wander at a push within their crowded, smelly, stuffy environment. Others are exposed to a certain amount of outside ground, which is known as free range which is a vast improvement to those housed indoors. Methods of factory farming not only expose the chickens to a life of living hell, but also expose them, and ultimately us, to the spread of diseases. It is a method of farming that treats the chicken as a piece of dead flesh, even before it is dead. It dehumanises the human, it gives vent to the Ego that feeds off the suffering of other sentient creatures. It is a method of farming that is open to fraud and careless action as discovered in the summer of 2017 when millions of eggs around the EU were found to be contaminated by an insecticide harmful to human health. [32]

According to the animal welfare organisation, PETA "Chickens are arguably the most abused animals on the planet." [33] From tiny bundles of yellow fluff to the day of slaughter they suffer. Egg laying hens will have part of their sensitive beaks cut off to stop them pecking each other out of sheer frustration of their unnatural confinement. In a natural state, a chicken can live between seven and ten years depending on its ownership and living conditions. But the life of a battery hen can be reduced to less than two, ending its days bruised and literally, battered, sometimes crippled, and devoid of strength and good health. Chickens destined for meat are treated no better. They are fed with drugs to make them grow fast and fat, beyond reasonable natural growth, putting huge strain on their internal organs, making them susceptible to heart attacks, organ failure and crippling leg deformities. While millions of male chicks that are neither good for egg laying, nor producing flesh for the meat industry are said to be ground up alive or tossed into bags to suffocate. Whereas battery hens at the end of their lives, their suffering and stress continues, cramped in small crates once again for their journey to the slaughterhouse, many dying on the way from stress or sustaining broken legs or wings from rough handling. In the USA, while completely conscious, in the slaughterhouse, the legs of the chickens are forced into shackles, their throats cut, and they are immersed in scalding hot water to remove their feathers. This process is such a fast-moving operation, many chickens miss the throat cutter and are literally scalded to death in the feather removal tanks.[34]

Other methods of slaughter involve the shackled, conscious chicken passing through water that is electrically charged thus stunning the bird first, before its throat is cut. UK law states, that all animals must be stunned before having their throats cut, thus many chickens, hens and turkeys are now killed using gas. This involves the birds remaining in their transport crates when placed in a gas chamber, thus avoiding handling, and shackling live birds, so to this extent, does have some welfare advantages. [34] Nevertheless, it does not cancel out the way we treat these sentient creatures during their lifetime. The world they are forced to be born into, bears no resemblance to the world my own poultry have lived in. Nor does it bear any resemblance to the world their natural instincts cry out for. We need to learn from previous generations, like my grandparents. Back then, in the 1940s and 1950s, a lot of families kept hens in their back garden, a throwback to generations before then who lived a more natural, sustainable life. Granny's hens, like mine were lucky, they had an orchard, and fields to wander in. And when their time came to be in the "pot," after their egg laying days were over, granny would wander out to the orchard, gather up her chosen victim, place a brown paper bag over its head, inducing calm, tuck the hen under her arm, and with one twist of her wrist, the neck was broken. Within a few seconds the hen was dead. It had not suffered a barbaric life. It had not suffered a barbaric journey to the slaughterhouse. It had not suffered a barbaric death.

It is hardly surprising that grandad, and probably many other farmers who farmed traditionally, built up a close relationship with their cows. For science now demonstrates that cows share 80% of their genes with humans. [35] And so, we are linked, not just Spiritually, but genetically too. Which is why the medical profession can now take body parts from the cow such as heart valves for human heart surgery. Cows are one of the most important animals used by Man. We use them for meat, milk, cheese, butter, and cream. We use them for clothing, for furnishings in our homes and cars. We use them to furnish our feet. Even non-edible by-products are used for the human world. Such as the intestines which are used to make tennis racket strings or strings for a musical instrument. Or the bones that are ground up and used in the formation of bone China. Or extracting a protein called keratin from the hooves to make a special fire extinguishing foam, now used by airport fire and rescue teams across the world. Industrial companies around the world have devised very clever ways of taking inedible parts of cows, pigs, sheep, and horses and converting them into consumer items. Scientists in America have even started using pigs in controversial research whereby the pig is used as an "biological incubator" for growing human organs, such as pancreas, hearts, livers, kidneys, lungs, and corneas. [36] We take all our farm animals for granted in our commercial, materialistic world without giving a second thought that the commodities we use come from a sentient creature.

Factory farming is another way of describing intensive farming, usually of cows, pigs, turkeys, and chickens. Its aim is to produce massive quantities of meat, eggs, or milk at the lowest possible cost. Other areas of intensive farming include crops, fish, goats and the less talked about of animals, mink, fox, and rabbit. Yes, intensive farming of fur still exists under the radar, perfectly legal even within the EU. Animals suffer all over the world in the hands of Man, including in the name of science through the practise of vivisection. In factory farming, and the like, animals are incarcerated in artificial, sometimes horrendous conditions, separating them off from their natural environments, thus stifling their natural instincts. The harbingers of factory farming know what they are doing. They address pent-up emotions of the imprisoned animals, by clipping beaks of hens, and extracting teeth in piglets, without pain relief or anaesthetic, on the pretext of reducing aggressive behaviour from built-up frustration. Science has found that after disbudding, the heart rate of a calf is heightened, thus showing that pain was felt. And after teeth extraction, and the docking of its tail, the stress of its experience caused some piglets to die. Imagine how you would feel, incarcerated in a prison, physically tortured, packed with thousands of other people, in a windowless, artificial environment, where you never saw the sun, where you never breathed fresh air, where you received basic food and water, where you defecated in the same room? Thus, these animals suffer in silence from birth to death, it is a cruel, barbaric, and heartless way of rearing millions of animals for the consumption and use of an overpopulated world of human beings. Yet, we are constantly hearing in the UK and Ireland, how more people are becoming obese, a problem shared in other western countries too.

At the same time, mountains of food are wasted every year in the UK, apparently £17 billion's worth thrown in the bin, destined for landfill, which questions the need for producing all this food in the first place! [37]

In his book, "Farmageddon," Philip Lymbery has written a harrowing account of intensive, industrial farming around the world. It could be said, that Lymbery is also "reading" the energy of Spirit, Spirit within the individual sentient creature, and the collective Spirit of nature. He has disclosed the hidden barbaric cruelty, which is imposed upon the imprisoned animals, including fish, all of whom are forced to suffer in artificial and often filthy conditions. But this is not intended to be an emotional book although I found it so, and I daresay many others do as well. It is a factual book based on Lymbery's investigations of the global food industry. He and Isabel Oakeshott, a political journalist, have disclosed the myth that factory farming is efficient and healthy, not just for the animals involved, but for the public and the farmer who buy into it. He has revealed a method of farming that relies on chemicals and antibiotics to keep it going, a falsehood working against nature, thus impacting the world's biodiversity, ecosystems, the natural environments, and wildlife, putting all life on planet Earth at risk with new and mutating viruses and bacteria. There is growing evidence for the selection of antibiotic-resistant bacteria on these farms, which can persist in the meat, the eggs, and even make it directly to the human beings who keep them! As these bacteria reach into our society, they place all of us at risk of death from infections that can no longer be treated with antibiotics. Even vegetarians aren't safe, as manure used to fertilise lettuce and sprouts can contain antibiotic-resistant bacteria, and lead to serious food-poisoning outbreaks (about half of the E Coli outbreaks listed by the CDC in 2019 were from non-meat sources, despite E Coli being an animal bacterium!). One of the most famous such organisms, a simple E Coli urinary infection that was resistant to our "last resort" antibiotic colistin can be traced over the course of 15 years spreading from pig farms in China, through Europe, to North America. (https://sciencetrends.com/a-dangerous-antibiotic-has-traveled-around-the-world-from-china)

Lymbery has also disclosed that intensive industrial farming is perpetrated by mega commercial enterprises, fuelled by the notion of megabucks, justifying it to themselves and those that buy into it, that the world needs to be fed! [28] Yes, it does, but at what cost? Surely, one answer is to be more Mindful of what we eat and how much we eat, to go back to a more sustainable, natural way of life and to control our own numbers? During the Second World War, the people of Britain were asked to "dig for victory" as a means for the nation to feed itself. Perhaps this ethos is good for all nations today. But instead of digging for victory in a war between Homo sapiens, we should unite in "Digging for the Planet" to not only feed ourselves but refurbish and replenish what we have destroyed in the wild, to connect with nature again. For we are part of nature, not separate from it. Currently, our way of life and how we treat other animals is not sustainable. If the Ego continues to reign, Mother Nature will intervene, setting us back to begin again, if she so chooses! The 2020 pandemic with COVID-19 is perhaps the reality of this prediction that I was given several years ago from my Spirit guides, that Mother Nature would intervene. This virus, originating from bats but possibly passing through pangolins in a Chinese wet-market, is wholly unsuited for the human host – it spreads easily, but is also dangerous to the most vulnerable, and quickly proved itself unstoppable without draconian measures. Even as the cases and death toll rose, countries across the globe instituted lockdowns to curb the spread. During this period, it gave many people time to reflect on the problems with our modern society – how little time we spent with our families, how little time we spend with Nature. As travel and commerce plummeted, so did pollution levels. For a few brief months there was a thought among many that while they longed for things to "return to normal" they asked themselves what parts of "normal" were worth returning to?

Sadly, many people did not heed this lesson – with rare exceptions the lockdowns have failed, and cases continue to rise, as has pollution. Even the ban on wet markets, selling live animals for human consumption (or slaughtering them on-site), was temporary. I do not know what it would take at this point to convince Mankind that there needs to be better balance between our existence and that of the rest of the planet.

Anyone who has had a close relationship with their pets or works within animal husbandry or animal welfare occupations will know, as I do, that animals have feelings like us. They are conscious, thinking, living beings. It does not take a genius to see that animals feel pain, fear, and distress and conversely, can feel the opposite. It does not take a genius to observe that animals are conscious of themselves and their place within their environment. The idea that other animals are non-thinking, non-feeling, non-intuitive vessels go back to the philosopher René Descartes, who in the 17th century, argued that animals do not have consciousness. But this is far from the truth. Now thankfully, science is beginning to catch up with what Spirit taught me many years ago and my grandfather and many others like him also knew intuitively. On 7th July 2012, a group of prominent international neuroscientists signed the "Cambridge Declaration on Consciousness". Here it was asserted unequivocally that, "humans are not unique in possessing the neurological substrates that generate consciousness." "Nonhuman animals, including all mammals and birds, and many other creatures, including octopuses, also possess these neural substrates." The declaration was signed by the conference participants that very evening in the presence of Professor Stephen Hawking. [38]

We might hope, indeed presume, that having reached such ground-breaking conclusions from one of the finest academic institutions in the world, that attitudes in the public arena might change towards other sentient creatures, and other life in the natural world. But we would be wrong. Such important research is not privy to the public on a scale that it deserves. And so, the public continue to go about their daily lives, ignorant to the fact, that other sentient creatures suffer at their expense. Our relationship with planet Earth is now at crisis point. And how we treat other animals are intrinsically interwoven with this crisis. Intensive farming treats animals like commodities, unfeeling lumps of flesh, caught up in a world of consumerism where materialism rules, driven by economics and financial gain. Thus, factory farming raises ethical questions, the efficiency of food production, ignoring animal welfare, and the growing global population, ignoring the environmental impact and the risk to human and other animal health through overused antibiotics, antimicrobial agents, anthelmintics, hormones and vaccines, protein, mineral and vitamin supplements. ¬

Our secular materialistic world is now driven by the Ego, the commercial world of economics, banking, and financial institutions. With both farmer and consumer most often in hock with credit dept. and high mortgages, there is encouragement still further for mass production of cheap meat and other food. And so, the world population is now on a conveyor belt finding it difficult to get off. Relying on the artificial world of the supermarket which hides the artificial world of those who suffer in silence on our behalf. The materialistic world serves to act as a barrier between Man and nature, thus breaking down the sensitivities and considerations we should have, not only for the natural world and all other species within it, but also, for the sentient creatures we choose to control, incarcerate, and neglect in the name of homo sapient survival. As sentient creatures we share our world with, as creatures we rely so heavily on; surely, they deserve our respect, consideration, and compassion? The Homo sapient presumes superiority over other species, thus he should have more intellect to rise above such barbaric behaviour, taking into consideration what science now teaches us. But sadly, this is not the case, as witnessed in the world today. And yet the Spirit of Man and the Spirit of all Life on planet Earth cries out to be heard!

Chapter 13

Digital Brain

My parents purchased their first TV in the late 1950s. Standing about 3ft tall, it stood like a piece of teak furniture, a 12-inch screen implanted in the front near the top of the apparatus - a far cry from the flat-screen smart TVs we have today. However, it brought another view of the world into our daily lives despite only having two channels, with programs mostly aimed at adults. TV was a novelty in those days, very few people could afford one and those that did, like my family, put up with its foibles in the name of entertainment and broadening the mind. Children's programmes were thus considered less important. Dad loved it. He was an instant telly addict, becoming almost possessive of his new purchase. Working at the time in a drawing office as an electrical draughtsman, dad saw himself as being the only one in the family as being qualified to look after this technological advancement to the home. Which I always thought was strange, since mostly, "looking after it" seemed to involve just giving the telly a good thump on the top when the picture became blurred, fuzzy, or moved. This breakup of our TV picture happened when other electrical devices were being used by a neighbour or when a car drove past the house which happened quite frequently with our home being on a main route into town. I now know that the reasons for this interference on our television screen was caused because earlier pieces of electrical equipment were not fitted with filters and the ignition system of cars were not fitted with suppressors. Filters and suppressors were eventually introduced because it was found that all electrical equipment will generate some form of electromagnetic radiation. And electromagnetic radiation will "interfere" with other electrical signals.

Less than ten years later I was going out with a Cornishman. And being a Cornishman, he was always proud of the origins of his birth. From the moment we met, it was obvious he loved his homeland, describing to me the beautiful area in the Cornish countryside where his family still lived on a farm not far from the Atlantic coast. Having spent many happy childhood holidays in Cornwall, I had romantic memories of it and could not wait to meet his family and see his family home. When the time came for my first visit, I was both nervous and excited. At the time, we both worked in the illustrating department at Westland Aircraft in Yeovil and could leave work at 4:30 on a Friday afternoon. So, having prepared for our long journey the night before, our journey down to Cornwall began as soon as we left the office. The convenience of dual carriageways or motorways down to the West Country did not exist in 1967 which meant the journey was long and arduous, ensuring we did not reach Camborne until nearly 10 o'clock in the evening, long after it got dark. It was wet and cold and murky as befitting the North Cornish coastline in winter when it was hit with a driving heavy sea fret streaming off the Atlantic Ocean. With window-screen wipers madly working overtime, I shivered in my old Morris Minor as we travelled out into the countryside through twisty lanes. Now I was cold and hungry and tired. Then suddenly my boyfriend shouts, here we are, turn here. And so, I did, down a bumpy dirt track shielded on both sides with wind-blown high hedges bent over after years of attack from North winds funnelling us down to the farm. An outside light was on, shining from the front of the house and showcasing a farmyard and its barns. Despite the miserable weather, it all looked so natural and charming cloaked in semidarkness, and I could not wait to see it properly in daylight hours. After all the pleasantries of new introductions, I was shown to a room which I was sharing with my boyfriend's sister. Despite my exhaustion I found it difficult to sleep. The weather outside had got worse, lashing the house with heavy rain and gale force winds and the constant sound of a crackling, fizzing, and hissing noise. In the darkness, my bedroom companion sensed I was awake. I asked her, "what's that noise", and she said, "don't worry, it's the pylon outside, you'll soon get used to it!" But I never did.

I never imagined that the first thing I would see from the bedroom window in the morning was not a beautiful Cornish view, but a ghastly blot on the landscape, a giant electric pylon literally standing yards away from the house. Instantly and intuitively, I knew it was radiating bad energy, toxic energy which sounded out a warning when hit with wet conditions. Interestingly, I was told later by my boyfriend's father that when the pylon was first erected, the cows on the farm spent weeks afterwards mooing and hoofing the ground around it. It seemed I was not the only one to sense the bad energy! A year later, I married my Cornishman, and I was to learn over the years my mother-in-law suffered from dreadful debilitating migraines which would lay her up for several days. On one of our later visits, we found her still recovering from one. Looking completely washed out and feeling very delicate, she sat with me in the kitchen having a quiet cup of tea. Suddenly the kitchen was filled with a bright light which moved over to my mother-in-law completely engulfing her. She seemed totally unaware and so was her daughter who had come into the room. They were having a conversation, but I could not tell you about what. I was too busy "listening" to another! With goose bumps all over my skin, in my mind's eye I "saw" my paternal grandfather from the "other side", and I "heard" him say, "Electric pylons are dangerous." "The cables they carry radiate electromagnetic energy which is bad for the human brain." I have never forgotten my grandfather's warning and have learnt over the years that some people are more susceptible than others. Unfortunately, my new mother-in-law was of the latter which is why she suffered from migraines and why her guardian Angel was there trying to protect her with healing energy.

Years later, while working in our shop in the Northumberland village of Warkworth, a regular customer suddenly walked in beaming from ear to ear with her new-fangled communication aid, her mobile phone. It was 1993 and there were not many people in our village that owned mobile phones at that time. Certainly, nobody in our family did that we knew of. My stepdaughter was the first in our family to purchase a mobile phone, and that was a few years later. Now of course, it is said here in Ireland at least that over 90% of the population own one. But back in our shop, 25 years ago, the world of communication was only just on the brink of changing. Making the most of a quiet lull of our working morning, Mickey our customer was singing the virtues of her new purchase, explaining she had bought the same for her young daughter so they could stay in touch with each other when her daughter went horse riding. "I can't imagine why you haven't bought one" she said. "Mobile phones are so convenient"! "They release you to live life". Her words seemed to provoke an instant reaction. For suddenly I "saw" in my mind's eye my brother from "the other side" and I "heard" him "whisper" in my ear, "Don't buy one sis, these things are dangerous.". "They will make you feel ill, and cause cancer for some". To this day, my husband and I still do not own a mobile phone! Armed with warnings from the Spirit world, I treat all electronic devices with caution, moderation, and balance. But this is not so with the status quo, for as is the case with all modern inventions, the Homosapien puts all his eggs in one basket, cutting off communication through other sources and avenues, and thus according to Maryanne Demasi there are over 6 billion mobile phone subscribers worldwide, many of them smart phones with Wi-Fi functionality. [39] However, despite the widespread use of this technology, new data shows overall brain cancer rates have not increased giving credence to the argument that mobile phones are safe. But can we rely on this information? After all, it can take decades for brain cancer to develop and being rare, is unlikely to show up from data of the general population. Indeed, we could say, society has been down this route before with the tobacco industries. Here too it was claimed for decades that the product was safe while millions of people undermined their health and others died. Now we know categorically that smoking is detrimental to health causing many smoking related diseases and cancer. Of course, not everyone who smokes dies of cancer. And many people die of cancer who have never smoked. The same argument could be applied to mobile phone users etc. It is all a matter of our own personal DNA and our own acceptable levels of exposure to electromagnetic radiation. Some people like my ex-mother in-law and myself are susceptible, while others will be less so. But with our children now being exposed to high levels of electromagnetic radiation as never before, absorbing twice as much as that of an adult, is this new technology worth the risk? Personally, I feel caution and moderation in its use is the best approach. For I know from my Spiritual experiences and the information passed onto me thereof it will come to pass eventually, no matter how many years it takes, that the safety of mobile phones and other electronic devices is a fallacy purported by the marketing men, and those with vested interest in this new technology. Not only are we susceptible to the toxins of electromagnetic radiation causing potential brain tumours, {already statistics in the US show an increase in young adults} but we could also be susceptible to other health concerns related to overuse or over exposure to our electronic devices. Only recently in China, a woman had to undergo emergency surgery to remove blood clots having spent too much time in one position on her mobile phone! Apparently in China there has been an increase in young adults suffering from blood clots. [40] There is also growing concern that children and young adults are becoming addicted to their smart phones and/or to violent computer games, social media sites, or becoming targets for cyber bullying or paedophiles. Is there cause for concern? Has this new technology become addictive? Or is it simply becoming a way of life in accordance with our evolutionary progress? William Thompson's research suggests a bit of both·[41] We cannot stop our evolutionary progress, but neither should we become addicted to its tools and vehicles. Addiction to anything can undermine our physical, mental, emotional, psychological, and Spiritual health. For addiction is fuelled by the Ego, it is all consuming. And when the Ego is at work, we are separated from our sensory faculties, the coded language that hits our solar plexus, our higher consciousness, our Spirit. Thus, we are in danger of allowing the digital age to erode our physic sensory faculties, and when this happens, we lose direction, we lose sense of the "real" world and our relationship within it. And just like thousands of Irish children who have online conversations with strangers, [42] as a species, we do not see the dangers we are in, we are in a sleep state, thus not only undermining our own survival, but that of the planet and all other Life thereof. The digital age is developing and exposing an indifference to Life.

As a Spiritual medium and healer, I have learnt through my mediumship experiences, that the energy of the mind can travel. It is far-seeing and far-reaching, it can transmit information through time and space, it knows no boundaries. Spiritual mediumship teaches me the energy of the mind, our thoughts can still communicate what they know after our physical demise. Thus, I have come to learn that the human brain, which generates its own electricity, albeit in small amounts, is a superior component to any man-made computer, and is simply a component that houses the mind. Over time, the mind, our thoughts, have evolved and developed their ability to reason through analytical thinking. Nevertheless, at a deeper level, there are many people like me out there that still retain the frequencies of their psychic, telepathic faculty, the ability to read the energies around us, the coded language of our inner GPS that enables us to read the energies of our environment, and all Life thereof. The coded language of Spirit, a consciousness within us and around us, and above us, is really a form of energy that links us as one humanity, and to all Life. Thus, we are all susceptible to a greater or lesser extent to overexposure of electromagnetic radiation caused by our electronic devices.

You may question what the spiritual medium has come to know, that we can communicate telepathically, but now Prof Digby Tantam, Clinical Professor of Psychotherapy at the University of Sheffield, believes that our empirical physical language plays only a small part of how human beings communicate with each other. The Professor claims he can prove human telepathy, which he believes operates like Wi-Fi, sending and receiving signals all the time. This communication is the hidden coded language of our gut feelings, our intuition, those uncomfortable feelings we sometimes get in a crowded room, and mob mentality. [43] In other words, it could be said, the Professor is underwriting what the Spiritual Medium already knows, and that is, thoughts are energy, and they travel born of our capacity to communicate telepathically. If we continue to rely on electronic devices in our daily lives, we risk losing or damaging our own inner GPS, our psychic prowess, those gut feelings that warn us of danger, our intuition, the coded language of our Spirit leaving us more susceptible to the negative energies of the Ego. For the Spirit and the Ego utilise the telepathic faculty. We also risk losing, according to some health professionals, the ability to interact with each other on a human level, to engage emotionally and/or mentally in the real world. Of course, these concerns also apply to all mammals whose brains are electrical components and can also communicate telepathically, both with us and each other. The more developed the brain, the more developed the electrical and telepathic frequency. And like the cows all those years ago on my ex-father-in-law's farm, they too are susceptible to the general smog of electromagnetic radiation now all around us in the modern world.

It is a fact well-known to physicists and people qualified in Electronics that when electricity moves it will generate and transmit electromagnetic radiation. It is this electromagnetic radiation that is detected by a passive electrode when placed on the outside of the skull when EEG is performed. The EEG records the electrical signals passing around the brain by detecting the electromagnetic radiation generated by these micro-currents of the brain. Thus, it is known that small electrical signals can be affected by received electromagnetic radiation. Never in human history has our brain been so bombarded with the frequencies of electromagnetic radiation as it is today. Electromagnetic radiation is all around us in the natural world. All living things are surrounded by their own electromagnetic field. As a Spiritualist, we know it as our aura. It is nature's way of protecting us by sending out signals we can learn to read it is part of our innate GPS. But now we are bombarded by the frequencies of electromagnetic radiation radiating out from man-made devices, which far from protecting us is detrimental to our health and well-being. We now live in a fast-moving world, in a society governed by electricity. Thus, generating a need for more pylons carrying increasing numbers of electrical cables which radiate ever increasing levels of electromagnetic radiation feeding into the development and growth of the digital electronic age. Thus, generating a need for the development of ground stations or mobile masts which also radiate even more levels of electromagnetic radiation enabling communication between our Wi-Fi's, our computers, smartphones, tablets, and smart TVs to take place. Mobile phones, Wi-Fi's and all our computer devices and other electrical equipment either by design or by accident will generate electromagnetic radiation. Thus, when you put your mobile phone to the side of your head you risk the electromagnetic radiation "interfering" with the electrical signals of your brain, putting at risk our own inner GPS, our telepathy, our intuition, in much the same way we used to get interference on our TV screens. The same happens when you sit in front of your computer or close to your Wi-Fi system for too long. And so, our electronic age with all its conveniences is now ruling human existence engulfing all of us in the smog of electromagnetic radiation. And now science and some health professionals are catching up with what Spirit has been informing me for many years, and that is electronic devices radiate electromagnetic radiation which puts our well-being at risk, our psychic/Spiritual, emotional, mental, and physical health.

Now of course, smart phones and other electronic devices have become a way of life for billions of people globally. They are likely to remain a significant part of both material and normative culture, evolving into more powerful and convenient forms of everyday technology. Financially and economically, it is worth billions for governments around the world. The structure of our culture and society has changed beyond all recognition to what it was 25 years ago. Now the digital age rules leaving very little room to manoeuvre outside its perimeter. And so, we must take stock of what we are doing to our brains. If we wish to continue living in a world of electronic technology and all its conveniences thereof, we must understand and become aware of the workings of this technology, its side-effects, the potential health hazards Spiritually, psychologically, emotionally, mentally, and physically, and what we can do to protect ourselves. For a start, we do not have to put all our eggs in one basket. In other words, we do not have to rely on our smart phones, laptops, or computers to interact with each other and the wider world. The world worked and still does in wondrous ways long before this invention. It is time to give our brains and minds a break before it is too late! It is time to protect the next generation, our children. It is often our children that put our lives into perspective. And it often takes a disaster in life to help us see through the trivia stuff we consider important. Dr Alistair McAlpine, a palliative paediatrician in South Africa was fed-up with seeing negative stories appearing on his twitter account. And so, he decided to share the positive and inspiring thoughts of the terminally ill children under his care. When the doctor asked about their wishes and their reflections on life none of the children wished they had watched more TV. None of them wished they could spend more time on Facebook. In fact, many of the older children wished they had spent less time worrying about what other people thought. None of them enjoyed fighting with others. None of them enjoyed being in hospital. Their greatest wish was that they could have more time with their families. Nearly all the children loved books and wished their parents had read to them more often. They loved people who made them laugh. They enjoyed friendships that valued them. They loved board games, playing with, or cuddling up to their favourite pet. They loved cuddling up to their teddies at night. They loved ice cream, picnics, and family time. They valued kindness and close relatives like their grandparents. Heartbreakingly many of the children worried about how their parents would cope after they had passed away. These stories were so touching, the doctor's Twitter thread went viral indicating to me the core of those who read these accounts, the Spirit within was touched and awakened to the reality and Truth and meaning of life. [44]

Addicted to the digital age, many people now fear life without it. But it is a fallacy and a falsehood shielding them from real-life and what really matters. It takes a terminally ill child to make you see that. What these children were teaching us was the value of sincere friendships. Not so-called friendships on a social media site - but the value of engaging with each other on an emotional, mental, or physical level. The value of quality time with people we love, which we find very often too late, to be priceless. These children were teaching us that the material world holds no comfort. In the end, what really matters is kindness, caring and love, humility and compassion and the importance of engaging with each other in the physical world. So, put down your smart phones, your tablets, leave them behind. Lock them in a drawer or cupboard for a day or two. Treat yourself to an electronic digital free weekend. Nourish the mind with good food, conversation, emotional and mental interaction on a physical level. Have a family day out, go to the beach, the countryside, the park, take the dog for a walk, have a picnic. Have fun, laugh, and play, eat ice cream. Get involved with activities with friends and/or family. With the children, read to them and get them to read to you! Play board games. Cherish every moment of your human life, get back to nature, become mindful of other species around you, become mindful of the beautiful world, go gardening, touch the soil, breathe in the fresh air. Take a camera (no not your smart phone!), record those special memories, make a family photo album, something physical and tangible to treasure. Concentrate on enjoying and appreciating the simple things in life. Go for a digital free holiday. Be kind, generous and loving in thought and deed. Allow your Spirit within to glow igniting a rippling effect, touching everything else around you with positive feel-good digital-free energy.

Chapter 14

War Cry

As a young mum, back in the late 1970s, {and a closeted Spiritual medium and healer at the time,} I was naturally inclined to instil into my children the value of peace and harmony among all humanity. I thus never felt comfortable allowing my children to play games, read books or watch TV programmes of a violent nature. Even such innocent programs as "The Dukes of Hazard" or the "A Team" acting out the struggle between good and bad were monitored. As far as I was able, I discouraged any link to violence coming into the home, which included purchasing toys that represented any type of weapon for my children to play with. However, this didn't stop my young sons, Nicholas, and Daniel, playing cowboys and Indians in the back garden. Their jeans tucked into the top of their little wellies and Daniel wearing an old straw hat of mine with twigs stuck in their waistbands to be used as "pretend guns" shooting "pretend bullets" at each other from behind the apple trees.

These halcyon days, and the innocence of their play was in sharp contrast to the reality of what real guns can do. Not only destroying lives, but destroying the network of families and society, leaving them damaged psychologically, mentally, and emotionally as witnessed so often in America these days. Where my sons got the idea of guns and cowboys and Indians shooting each other, I never did find out with any certainty. Probably from Playschool or school, and the other children they played with. I came to realise, in the end, there is only so much we can do to protect our children. We can't wrap them up in cotton wool, it would be cruel and irresponsible to do so. They need to be taught there is violence out there. But they should also be taught that violence is wrong. It screws you up, psychologically, mentally, and emotionally, impacting the central nervous system, impacting the Spirit, the Soul of oneself. Thus, contributing to health concerns thereof not only for the victim, but also for the perpetrator and the families involved, while at the same time having a rippling effect on the wider community.

These days our children are exposed to all levels of violence from a very early age, not only through TV programmes and social media sites, but through computer games, where war and violence is portrayed as entertainment, blurring the demarcation to what is acceptable and what is not in a civilised society for those that are susceptible. Indeed, we see violence portrayed as entertainment in sport, such as in boxing. As the crowd cheers and bay for blood at a boxing arena, it is not difficult to imagine how the crowds used to bay for blood during Roman times when the lions were set free into the arena to tear the Christians apart. Some people would argue, we have come a long way since those days. We are now more civilised and enjoy our sport under regulated controlled conditions. But I can't help wondering, we haven't come far, as I witness members of the audience standing up, cheering their favoured boxer on as the opponent hits the deck, his face covered in blood and bruises, risking his life with a damaged brain. But the audience care-not for the injuries. Instead, the injuries excite the adrenaline and lust for more blood. And when Man is not baying for the blood of another Man, he is baying for the blood of another species, all in the name of sport, some legal, and some illegal activities. And so, we no longer just pick up snippets of violence on our TV news programs or in our newspapers. Now we are exposed to it 24/7, either through our TV networks or electronic devices informing us of some violent action from anywhere around the world, desensitising society's sensitivities towards it, thus unwittingly making violence an acceptable way of life. Indeed, globally, men, women and children suffer violent domestic abuse in silence on a regular basis. In the UK alone, official crime figures for 2012/13 revealed more than 1. 1 million women and 720,000 men had been victims of this insidious crime, some may even lose their lives in an act of murderous rage, very young children being the more likely victim of the latter.

And so, it comes as no surprise to learn in recent times, as they lose ground and control in war-torn Islamic states, the terrorist group Isis are said to be using the Internet to radicalise young people, urging them to commit atrocities in the name of their warped interpretation of the Muslim faith. Our computers and the Internet are marvellous inventions, bringing huge benefits into our lives, to be used as a tool for the benefit of humanity, our higher consciousness, our Spirit. But the Ego is always there, the lower consciousness, always on the lookout for a tool to exert its negative influence. And so, the Ego of young people, mostly young men become soft targets for the perverted ideology of the Ego of terrorist groups. Our electronic devices and the Internet are now used widespread and commonly as a tool for the underbelly of society, advertising, and/or encouraging acts of violence, criminality, and/or communicating intimidation or abusive language or images of sexual abuse, the worst atrocity being against young children. The Ego, the primitive side of Man, still seeks to satisfy its lust for negative outlet, always looking for recruits, violence being the crème de la crème of all passions and urges thereof.

Human history is well documented down through the ages of violent confrontation, hostilities at all levels beginning with stones and rocks, developing into spears, knives, and axes, before developing more "sophisticated" weapons such as canon, guns and now nuclear arms. Not content with Man-to-Man combat or tribe to tribe, we can now deploy weapons of mass destruction vaporising huge cities and millions of people with the press of a button. We have a beautiful planet, but contentment and responsibility seem to evade the very essence of Man for many people. We have ambitions to fly to other planets, while we have the capacity to destroy what we already have through nuclear warfare. It seems innate of Man, that if he doesn't have a reason, he'll soon find one, to knock seven bells out of his neighbour. Usually, it's to have power over another, either another Man, another continent or country on the back of religious and/or political differences. In commemorating the dead of the First or Second World War, we often hear in the speeches of the heads of state, "We must never let this happen again". But since those times, over the last 70 years, the world has witnessed many conflicts where millions of people have suffered or lost their lives. For example, soon after the Second World War with the collapse of British imperialism, came the partition of India, where the population, diverse in its religions, had lived peacefully together for thousands of years until the British colonial masters intervened, along with indigenous politicians who had ambitions of their own. And so, along with India's independence, the two self-governing countries of Pakistan and India came into existence in August 1947. Thus, separating Hindu and Muslim majorities off from each other, displacing millions of people from areas they had called home for generations, setting neighbours and friends against each other in overwhelming acts of violence and bloodshed.

We have also witnessed the Korean War, {July 1950/July 1953} which has never officially ended, which is why North Korea is now so determined to protect itself with nuclear weapons, and why tensions still exist between North and South and their allies, America, and China accordingly. Another war between North and South was the Vietnam War, {November 1955/April 1975} lasting over 19 years, involving the Soviet Union and China which allied with the North, while the United States, South Korea, Australia, and Thailand allied with the South. Collectively, from both sides of the divide, millions of lives were lost amid human atrocities whether defending communism or democracy. So, who is to say, who is good and who is evil? For within the human condition, we all have an Ego and a Spirit. So, it could be argued, both the political ideologies of communism and democracy will have the wherewithal to harbour both. For in the end, it is down to the individual. We are not judged by our politics, our ideologies, our religion, our language, our gender and/or skin colour. We are judged by the fallout of our Ego, and the workings of our Spirit. The Ego is the warlord, but like all warlords is arrogant, selfish, ambitious, pompous, full of its own importance. While at the same time, is weak willed, easily led, indoctrinated, radicalised, or brainwashed, perverted. Whereas the Spirit is a tough cookie, unyielding and untouched by other persuasions. It stands alone in its purity, yet united and linked into Spirit of all humanity, and all living things on earth, which in turn, is linked into the greater Universal Spirit which some of us call God. However, the nature of Man is such, that anyone perceived as different is viewed under a cloak of suspicion, not to be trusted, to be feared, to be rooted out. Once Man has targeted his enemy, he can then justify to himself all manner of barbarism and suffering, even to the sick, the weak, the elderly, women, and children.

Considered to be one of Europe's deadliest conflicts since the Second World War, the breakup of the former Yugoslavia {March 1991/November 2001} was marked by many war crimes, including ethnic cleansing, crimes against humanity and rape. While the dissolution of the old Soviet Union in December 1991 brought about war and civil unrest between and within the different states that claimed independence. {On 24th February 2022 the Russian President Vladimir Putin gave orders to his military machine to invade his neighbour Ukraine with the false justification that he's saving the people from a Neo Nazi regime. But like all illogical madmen, he's killing thousands while millions are leaving their country, their homeland being destroyed. NATO and the West are paralysed with the threat of nuclear war. See footnote.} Thus, it appears that a tribal instinct in Man is rooted within his psyche, the Ego always ready to defend what he perceives as his, as witnessed in Africa over hundreds of years. The list of civil wars that have prevailed within this beautiful continent right up to the present day are too numerous to name, creating civil unrest, bloodshed and suffering to its populations, ravaging its lands, thus creating starvation. And not content with civil warfare, the African people exert violence on its wildlife for marginal profit to the indigenous people, satisfying the Ego of wealthy hunters of the West or feeding the addiction of ivory in China and/or the black market, either for ornaments or the misguided notion that ivory has medicinal properties. Only in recent times has the troubles of Northern Ireland come to a perceived end after three decades of violence between the Catholic and Protestant population. Although there has been some improvement since the 1998 Good Friday Agreement, sectarianism and religious segregation still exist under a cloak of normality and suspicion along with sporadic violence.

It seems that once war and violence, hatred and hostility take its grip, it gets passed down from one generation to the next, like the Civil War in Colombia which has lasted over 53 years. A peace deal was signed in October 2016 between the warring factions, but nevertheless it remains an uneasy peace. And although there has been a general reconciliation between Israel, Egypt and Jordan, Israel, and Palestine, after 50 years of conflict with loss of life and suffering on both sides, still struggle to reconcile their differences. Like the vultures that can hone into a corpse, the Ego can hone into a good war and once engagement takes place, the Ego doesn't leave until the bones are bare. And so, conflict becomes a way of life for generations of children who grow up knowing nothing else, damaged mentally, emotionally and psychologically, either to go through life burdened with their tainted memories and/or to take up the cudgel thrown down by the Ego of previous generations to go on committing acts of atrocity in time immemorial.

And so, we see the suffering of the innocent perpetrated by the Ego, if not born of religious and/or ethnic discrimination, then born of the political ambitions of heads of state. As seen in the wars of Afghanistan, {October 2001/present} and Syria {March 2011/present.} and Yemen {January 2015/present} which have their roots in political instability, sparking civil war between different factions escalating with international involvement, thus the latter operating a sort of proxy world war on someone else's soil! Other times, brothers fight brothers, speaking the same language, wearing the same-coloured skin, just having different opinions on politics or religion! Thus, it can be seen, that war and violence is endemic within the human condition. The Ego is always finding reasons to rage, seeking violent confrontation with an individual and/or the animal kingdom and/or with the wider world. Thus, for many people, war and violent conflict is a way of life. And for those that are addicted to violence, or don't have it for real, seek it out in entertainment.

Thus, violence becomes an addiction, it's the underbelly of society, it's the language of the Ego. It can be perpetrated behind closed doors, in the home, in the office, in the school, on the streets. It can turn into global conflict, on a scale never known before! And if not physical violence, then the violent assault on the senses created by intimidation and/or mental and/or emotional abuse. These acts of violence, whether physical, mental, or emotional can sap the energy, it demoralises the victim, the perpetrator and society. It undermines confidence which in turn instils a sense of fear, which in turn roots us all to the spot, stunting our ability to move forward in life. In war, the demarcation between the Spirit and the Ego becomes blurred leaving the way open for all sorts of atrocities to be committed. Which is why rape and/or violent intimidation against innocent victims such as women and children become easy targets in acts of perverted power over another, thus instilling fear into the wider community to control thereof. The perpetrator of violence is often a cowardly person, the bully in the home, in school and/or on the street who uses violence as a tool to inject a feeling of superiority and power within themselves, which is why atrocities have been known to be committed on the battlefield. Once the perpetrator connects with the perverted power of the Ego, given enough reign, the Spirit is ignored, it's plaintive weeping submerged.

Thus, on their return, many soldiers struggle with "normal life" again having witnessed and/or committed an act of violence. Thus, violence not only leaves the victim traumatised, but very often those that have witnessed it, or participated in it, scarred not just physically, but more importantly, psychologically, mentally and/or emotionally which we now recognise as post-traumatic stress. Returning soldiers from the First and Second World War did not have the luxury of battle-scarred counselling. It wasn't until the aftermath of the Vietnam War, where so many brutal atrocities were committed, leaving many returning soldiers scarred for life, was post-traumatic stress identified. It is now medically recognised as an acceptable mental disorder that can develop within anyone following exposure to violence and/or a traumatic event. Events, not just through warfare, but events such as sexual assault, traffic collisions, physical assault, abuse, or threats to a person's life. Trauma, violence, conflict and/or war thus reduces us to Walk in the Dark of the Ego, overwhelming the Spirit with mental and/or emotional pain, stunting growth, hindering development and the aptitude to move forward in life. And like a cancer it spreads, eating into the individual and/or society at large, which in turn can impact the wider world.

When we turn on our TV to watch the evening news, it is easy to think that the world is full of the "Walking Wounded". But there is hope, the Spirit might weep, but it cannot be broken. Spirit cannot be destroyed because it is directly linked into the Universal Spirit, our creator, the overwhelming force, omnipresent, omni-powerful, the greatest good of which all life is linked into. And as always, it's passively fighting back! For while we might witness the atrocities of the Ego, reducing us to Walk in the Dark, we also witness the upsurge of the Spirit, which only Walks in the Light. For Spirit makes itself known worldwide through peaceful demonstration for its revulsion for racial, religious, ethnic and gender discrimination. For its revulsion for abuse of any sort, intimidation, terrorism, war, conflict, and violence thus highlighting the higher consciousness of Man our Spiritual Self coming to the fore.

When we psychologically, mentally, and emotionally fight for the planet and all life thereof, we are Walking in the Light. When we psychologically, mentally, and emotionally fight for the climate, the environment, the natural world, and all species thereof, we are Walking in the Light. When we psychologically, mentally, and emotionally fight for the needs of others, we are Walking in the Light. When we show love, and if not love, because it is difficult sometimes, then kindness and compassion, we are Walking in the Light. When we show empathy for those less fortunate than ourselves, we are Walking in the Light. For to understand each other, we must learn to walk in each other's shoes, moving together forward as one humanity. Putting aside suspicion, ambition, greed, and lust. Putting aside vengeance and violence, intimidation, and bully tactics. Quailing the thirst of the Ego, then we are Walking in the Light, thus glowing from the inside out, radiating benefits, not only for those we touch, but ultimately to the wider world. Thus, activating the happy chemical of serotonin, not only within ourselves, but more importantly, within others, contributing to feelings of well-being and happiness to our shrinking world.

Now in my seventies, I know from personal experience of having an abusive mother what physical, mental, and emotional abuse can do to you. Later in life, unresolved emotional and psychological issues contributed greatly to two emotional and nervous breakdowns on the back of matrimonial failure. I have heard it said that an abused child is marked for life. And it is true. Either the Ego will rise again to repeat the same old patterns. Or, with the right guidance, which I have always had from the Spiritual Realm, my innate Spiritual sensitivities were heightened, thus I have always known that violence has no place in a civilised society. Violence begets violence, as seen in the UK recently with rising knife crimes amongst youngsters as young as 10 years old, who seek to be "someone" within a gang. The mindset who wage war pitting country against country, brother against brother is an extension of tribal or gang warfare, which is an extension to violence perpetrated against an individual. It's about having power and control over another, fuelling the Ego of the perpetrator giving vent to an uncivilised world, fuelling yet more Ego atrocities. With the Spirit submerged or ignored, no one wins! Currently, the Angels tell me that the human species are at a crossroads. We can either give full reign to the Ego leading to extinction of all species, including ourselves, and total annihilation. Or we can give full reign to our Spirit, so that one day in the distant future, as Man evolves on his Spiritual Path, he will come to learn the Truth of the lessons I have learnt.

Foot note.

Please note, events and dates were gleaned from the Internet and have not been verified and as such, are here only for the demonstration of Man's Ego. This chapter was originally written in 2015 but was not chosen by my editor to be included in this book, so I'm afraid to say, it has not been professionally edited. As I am quite close to self-publishing it, it's going out as it is. So please excuse any grammatical, punctual, and historical errors.

At 4:30 am on the 24th of February 2022 I was woken-up by my Spirit squad with the words "War Cry" penetrating my mind. I sensed the urgency in their call and heard them tell me, it must be included in this book. It is not unusual to be woken-up out of deep sleep by my Spirit squad. In fact, it's become so common over the years that I now keep a note pad and biro on my bedside table. I reached for these items; and scribbled "War Cry" then fell back under my duvet and into a deep sleep. It was only later during the day, I switched on Sky News to take away the boredom as I dusted the furniture in our lounge. My heart sunk when I heard the presenter announce that Putin had invaded Ukraine around 6 o'clock in the morning. I knew instantly why I had been woken-up so early that day with such urgency, and why my Spirit squad wanted this chapter to be included in this book.

Chapter 15

In the Beginning

By "Walking in the Light" we understand that Spirit is the essence of all creation, interlinked and interconnected. In the beginning there was a spark, an energy, an immaterial force - which over time developed into Life itself became individualised but nevertheless still linked by what came before. Thus, it is a consciousness, a Spirit Force, although not all creation is conscious of it. Where there is consciousness and awareness, an instinct propels itself forward into a greater complexity of Life and where Life develops, so does a different worldview. Man developed too, the twin aspects of Spirit and Ego.

This energy of consciousness, a Spiritual Force weaves itself through all creation. Some aspects of Life such as sentient creatures strengthen their consciousness with "a knowing" - an instinct, or intuitive psychic ability impregnated with memory of the infinite life thereof, and enabling communication with the past, the present and the future. It is the coded language of this Spiritual Force that has developed over time unique to all creation, but even more so to sentient creatures, and other animals on planet Earth. This consciousness pervades Life, now recognised by prominent international neuroscientists. [45] When we come to understand we are energy, we can come to understand that our thoughts can travel, they cannot be contained they can travel through space and time as can information and memory within the mind. The brain, as the computer to the Soul and the Ego works to communicate what is in the mind via telepathic means and what is in one mind can be shared and understood by another. The Ego, the great illusionist, the great pretender tunes into negative energies. Whereas our Spirit will only tune into energies of the highest good. It is according to Prof. Digby Tantrum our own Wi-Fi system,[46] or what I call, our own GPS, and without it we are nothing. If we continue to live in accordance with Ego incentive objectives we will literally lose direction in Life, submerging the Spirit while the Ego rules which is why currently Homo sapiens are in such a mess, impacting the planet and all its species with detrimental effect.

All my life I have "heard" voices and received visitations in my mind's eye. Information and messages have been conveyed to me via Spirit from the living world and those that have gone before. I now know through my research I am not alone. I believe there are millions of people like me around the world that still retain their innate psychic and intuitive abilities, and a telepathic faculty that developed over millennia from this Super Consciousness. The Universal Spirit enables us, including many other animals, we share our DNA with to communicate like a two-way radio or to tune into other energies within the environment. This psychic faculty which facilitates the Spirit can also find expression through vehicles of dance, music, painting, writing, poetry, sculpture, design, ceramics, pottery, in fact, any creative genre.

But it is often the case that to take on board such knowledge finds opposition. The trouble is, with the demise of orthodox religion and the advancement of conventional science and medicine, along with the technology juxtaposed with our secular world, the human species has become conditioned and indoctrinated to dismiss any belief in a Spiritual essence. Such thoughts are a nonsense or a sign of mental illness. And yet, it does not have to be like this. For conventional science like religion is limited and blinded by its own dogma. We still have much to learn. For example, science now explains the universe as energy but much of that energy is dark matter which cannot be even readily detected never mind explained. Even quantum physics, the pinnacle of scientific enquiry, has not resolved the big questions of who we are and where do we come from. What is the nature of reality? Questions that even Darwin (who began to doubt his own theory) and later the philosopher Thomas Nagel, and biologists Stuart Kauffman and Robert Reid could not resolve. [47] The British physicist James Jeans concluded that the universe "begins to look more like a great thought than a great machine" that exists "in the mind of some external Spirit", and Max Planck who wrote, "all matter originates and exists only by virtue of a force which brings the particle of an atom to vibration and hold this most minute solar system of the atom together." "We must assume behind this force the existence of a conscious and intelligent Spirit", "This Spirit is the matrix of all matter." [47] Steve Taylor PhD, a lecturer of psychology at Leeds Beckett University UK, also writes "quantum physics shows you cannot separate science and spirituality." "They cannot exist without each other." "They are one and the same."[47]

I believe that once we take on board that all creation is an infinite energy that cannot be contained - a consciousness, an awareness, an instinct to Life, a Spiritual Force that began its existence from the same spark - then we begin to understand that all creation is linked by this universal energy. If one link goes missing or is damaged, it puts all other links at risk. It also helps us to understand that our thoughts are energy that can travel through space and time and why many people like me who still retain their innate psychic and telepathic faculty can link into the energies that have gone before and the energies prevailing in the environment. You may think me absurd, or out of my depth in matters I know nothing about and merely relying on my instincts and the coded language of Spirit to inform me of this vital Truth, but Taylor has explored the many tenants of a materialistic (i.e., scientific) understanding of creation against what he calls a "panspiritist" view of the world. This is the notion that Spirit, or consciousness, is the fundamental reality, and here I entirely agree with him. In his book, "Spiritual Science" Taylor argues that a "panspiritist" view of the world can solve many riddles that neither conventional science nor religion can answer and that once we accept this vision of a sacred and interconnected world, our world becomes more meaningful, purposeful, and beautiful. An awareness of Spirit urges us to be more respectful and compassionate towards planet Earth and all its Life, and as we ourselves evolve Spiritually, we will no longer see ourselves and other life as soulless biological machines. We will no longer view our world as "us" against "them" who are there to be exploited and abused.

Thus, I believe Homo sapiens are part of Super Nature which is Supernatural -a Super Consciousness, a Spirit Force which pervades all Life and the very fabric of planet Earth that is governed and regulated by cosmic law and order. Currently though the modern world is cocooned in a virtual reality bubble, buried in a concrete jungle, relying on digital communication, desensitised to the energies that pervade Life, and desensitised to the energies of the natural world and all other species that are crying out for help. The energies of the Ego prevail, putting all Life as we know it at risk. Perhaps our only salvation is "Walking in the Light" which not only might explain our world and our role within it, but it might just help to save it.

Bibliography

Chapter 1

[1] RTE news April 16th, 2012 {Southern Ireland's radio and television broadcaster. Raidio Teilifis Eireann}

[2] BBC News website. Monday, September 18th, 2006.

[3] Collins Dictionary online.

[4] "DMT; The Spirit Module" by Dr Rick Straussman. Publisher: Park Street Press. Dec. 2000. ASIN: B017QV0YN8.

[5] "Spiritual Science" by Steve Taylor. Watkins Publishing ISBN 978-178678-158-1

[6]"Hearing Voices Network" website. c/o Sheffield Hearing Voices Network, Limbrick Day Service, Limbrick road, Sheffield, S6-2PE

[7] "Angels in my Hair" by Lorna Byrne. Published by Century. 2008 HB ISBN.

Chapter 3

[8] Andrew Brown of the Guardian. His blog on O2/07/2012.

[9] The science website, Pravda 07/11/2005.

Chapter 4

[10] National Trust dowsing courses 2009

Chapter 5

[11] "Celtic Astrology" by Helena Patterson. Llewellyn publications. St Paul, Minnesota, 55164-0383, USA. First edition, second printing 1995.

[12] "The Dawn of Astrology" by Nicholas Campion. Publisher: Hambledon Continuum; an imprint of Continuum Books. 2008. ISBN: 978-1-84725-214-2.

[13] "A History of Western Astrology" by S.J. Tester. {pp.111/112} Publisher: Boydell Press; new edition. January 13th, 1999. ISBN-10: 0851152554. ISBN-13: 978-0851152554.

[14] "A History of Horoscopic Astrology". From the Babylonian Period to the Modern Age. {p.174} by James Herschel Holden.

M.A. F.A.F.A. Published by American Federation of Astrologers, Inc. First printing 1996 ISBN: 0-86690-463-8.

[15] "Supernature" by Lyall Watson. The natural history of the supernatural. P. 51. Published by Coronet books/Hodder paperbacks Ltd. ISBN 0 340 18833 2

[16] www.greenhouseto.com Futuristic plant production. Does the colour of light affect plant growth?

[17] "The Aromatherapy Bible" by Jill Farrer-Halls. {p. 264} published by Godsfield Press, a division of Octopus Publishing Group Ltd. 2005. ISBN-13: 978-1-84181-271-7. ISBN-10: 1-84181-271-4.

[18] "Astrology" by Jeff Mayo. Second edition 1979. {pp.155/156} "Teach Yourself Books". Publisher; Hodder and Stoughton Ltd. ISBN: 0-340-27744-0.

Chapter 6

[19] Harvard university researcher's meditation. The website "Collective Evolution".

https://wwwcollective-evolution.com/2014/12/11/harvard-study-unveils-what-meditation-lierally-does-to-the-brain

Chapter 10

[20] Cleopatra: Queen, Lover, Legend. By Lucy Hughes Hallett. The introduction. Publisher: Pimlico; new edition. 3rd August 2006. ISBN-10:1844139379 ISBN-13:978-1844139378

[21] Josephine: Desire, Ambition, Napoleon. By Kate Williams. Publisher: Arrow {5th June 2014. ISBN-10: 0009955142X ISBN-13: 978-0099551423

Chapter 11

[22] RTE. {Raidio Teilifis Eireann} 8th August 2017. Documentary on vulture funds.

[23] Globalisation in World History by A.G. Hopkins. Publisher: Pimlico. 3rd January 2002. ISBN-10:0712677402. ISBN-13: 978-0712677400.

Chapter 12

[24] ScienceDaily website. Animal welfare could be improved by new understanding of their emotions. December 3rd, 2014. Credit: Brian Squibb/QMUL. And could goats become our new best friend? July 5th, 2016. Research done at Queen Mary University London.

[25] Wiley online library. Japanese psychological research. "Attachment between humans and dogs". Research done by, Miho Nagasawa, Kazutaka Mogi and Takefumi Kikusui. First published; 16th September 2009.

[26] Scientific American website: "Is the Gaze from Those Big Puppy Eyes the Look of your Doggie's Love?" Research finds that sustained eye contact between a dog and its owner causes oxytocin to spike in both-but not so in wolves. What it means remains to be seen. By Julia Hecht April 16th, 2015.

[27] BBC "Countryfile Autumn diaries". Tuesday 31st of October 2017.

[28] "Farmageddon" the true cost of cheap meat. By Philip Lymbery with Isabel Oakeshott. Bloomsbury publishing plc.

First published 2014. This addition 2015. ISBN 978 1 4088 46346.

[29] The Huffington Post USA online. Neuroscientist research's the mental and emotional faculty of pigs. Reported by Arin Greenwood 06/15/2015.

[30] EU ban on battery cages. https://www.gov.uk/

[31] The World's Poultry Science Journal online.

[32] The Guardian online. Friday 11th of August 2017. 17: 23 BST Daniel Boffey in Brussels and Kate Connelly in Berlin.

[33] People for the Ethical Treatment of Animals website. https://www.peta.org

[34] RSPCA slaughter fact file website.

[35] Science online. www.sciencemag.org/news/2009/04/mooove-over-humans-cow-genome-here

[36] "Pigs become biological incubators" reported on June 6th, 2016, by Fergus Walsh, medical correspondence for the BBC.

[37] "£17 billion's worth of food thrown into the bin annually". Reported on BBC News 17th of November 2017.

[38] The "Cambridge Declaration on Consciousness". 7th July 2012. A declaration drawn up by a group of prominent international neuroscientists.

Chapter 13

[39] Guardian online. Mobile phones and brain cancer Maryanne The. "No evidence of health risk" is not the same as "safe". We exist in a sea of radiofrequency radiation never before seen in human history. Are we lab rats in an experiment with no controls? By Demasi. Monday 15th of The Feb. 2016. 23:00 GMT.

[40] Daily Telegraph. Friday, 16th of March 2018. "Woman almost died after using phone for 20 hours". By Neil Connor in Beijing. Additional reporting by Christine Wei. "Evidence of growing blood clots."

[41] University of South Carolina, Lancaster, USA. http://scholarcommons.sc.edu/ji Journal of ideology. Volume 38. Number one. Article 3. Date 9/29/2017. Smartphones: Addiction, or a Way of Life? Research done by William E. Thompson 8865136. Texas A&M University-Commerce. William.thompson@tamuc.edu Mica L. Thompson Texas A&M University- commerce, mica.thompson@tamuc.edu

[42] The Irish Independent. "Thousands of children chat to strangers online." By Katherine Donnelly. Tuesday 6th February 2018.

[43] http://www.telegragraph.co.uk/science/2018/01/06/wi-fi-connects-human-brains-explains-people-have-gut-feelings/ interview by Sarah Knapton, science editor with Prof. Digby Tantrum, clinical Professor of Psychotherapy at the University of Sheffield. 6th January 2018 9:30

[44] Alistair McAlpine, palliative paediatrician in Cape Town hospital, South Africa. https://twitter.com/AlastairMcA30

Chapter 15

[45] The "Cambridge Declaration on Consciousness". 7th July 2012. A declaration drawn up by a group of prominent international neuroscientists.

[46] Tantrum: clinical Professor of Psychotherapy at the University of Sheffield. 6th January 2018 9:30.

[47] pp 173/176 & 217/218 "Spiritual Science" by Steve Taylor. Watkins publishing.co.uk. ISBN 978 1 78678 158 1

Printed in Great Britain
by Amazon

23345128R00121